Mary A. M Hoppus

All the World's a Stage

Vol. III

Mary A. M Hoppus

All the World's a Stage
Vol. III

ISBN/EAN: 9783337051235

Printed in Europe, USA, Canada, Australia, Japan

Cover: Foto ©ninafisch / pixelio.de

More available books at **www.hansebooks.com**

ALL THE WORLD'S A STAGE.

A Novel.

BY

MARY A. M. HOPPUS.

> Some men's sins go beforehand to judgment, and some follow after.

IN THREE VOLUMES.
VOL. III.

LONDON:
SAMPSON LOW, MARSTON, SEARLE & RIVINGTON,
CROWN BUILDINGS, 188, FLEET STREET.
1879.

(All rights reserved.)

LONDON:
PRINTED BY WILLIAM CLOWES AND SONS,
STAMFORD STREET AND CHARING CROSS.

ALL THE WORLD'S A STAGE.

CHAPTER I.

Sir Andrew. Will either of you bear me a challenge to him?

Sir Toby. Go, write it in a martial hand; be curst and brief . . . if thou *thou'st* him some thrice, it shall not be amiss.—*Twelfth Night.*

THE progress of King Rail began to be very rapid about this time. He had long influenced elections; and now the Ministry were thinking it necessary to meddle with him, and Mr. Gladstone, the Vice-President of the Board of Trade, was understood to be engaged in pickling a very efficient rod wherewith to keep him in order, and especially to prevent his unduly oppressing his third-class passengers, whom he seemed disposed to treat as cattle and carry standing. Colonel Sibthorpe had moved for a return of the killed and wounded, and was well known to regard railroads as (along with the Chartists) the latest manifestations of Satan—a kind of English Juggernaut—for people had begun to commit suicide with his assistance; and a perfect hornets' nest had been raised about the ears of King Rail by the new Sunday excursions, which a reverend orator somewhat too forcibly described as "trips to hell at seven and sixpence per head." Moreover, a great deal of ill will was caused by the numbers of "young gentlemen with theodolites," who marched about the country by day (in friendly districts), and prowled by night (in hostile ones), carrying "long white sticks with bits of paper attached," as if they were stewards—as they were, of King Rail. These young gentlemen, by fair means or foul, by night or by day, surveyed your land, whether you would or no. They stuck neither at garden gates nor at house doors, and calmly ignored both the Briton and his castle. A friend of Colonel Sibthorpe woke one fine morning to find that the enemy had been abroad while he slept, and had planted a flag-staff at his very door.

But more than all, the railway "navigator" was dreaded, and with good reason. To be sure, he was generally an Englishman (when he was not an Irishman); but a locust by any other name would soon be as terrible, and the navigator was a human locust, who spoiled wherever he came. He worked like a horse, and lived like a pig. He spread disease, he corrupted the peasantry; he went out, four or five hundred strong, armed with spade and pickaxe, to fight the navigators of some other line. All sorts of crimes horrified the peaceful neighbourhoods whose quiet he invaded. He often worked on through the seven days of the week, and made up for the loss of his Sunday's holiday by an occasional burst of ferocity and drunkenness. Village innocence is at least as frail as was that of Adam and Eve in Paradise; village girls often left their homes to go and live with the navigators a life nearly as savage, and quite as heathenish, as if they had all been Hottentots. Labourers left their masters and turned navigators themselves for the sake of the high wages. The navigators herded together in huts and sheds, which they made for themselves in a very good resemblance to an African kraal—with perhaps somewhat laxer than African morals. For all this, the navigator was more to be pitied than blamed. He was hired by an under-ganger, who was hired by a ganger, who was hired by a contractor, who made one fortune out of his contract with the company, another out of the "tommy shop"— where the navigator was obliged to buy bad food very dear with the tickets issued in advance—and a third, when, on the collapse of the company, he snapped up the land itself. A very few contractors, like Peto and Jackson, paid weekly in money, provided decent shelter, encouraged sick clubs, and made arrangements for religious instruction; and were rewarded by their men staying with them for as many as fifteen years together, and behaving soberly and orderly. But the great majority of the contractors made haste to be rich, and cared no more for the navigator than for the pickaxe he wielded. It was the ambition of a navigator of the superior sort to save a little money and become an under-ganger, and then a ganger—perhaps even a contractor; and thus, when the crash came, it sometimes happened that the first were last, and the last first, with a vengeance.

But if King Rail had many enemies, his friends were also many. He was preached upon from the pulpit. Ezekiel had prophesied of him. He was extolled above the pyramids of Egypt and the aqueducts of Rome. His health was drunk at feasts. Princes and peers vied with each other to do him honour. My Lord Marquess of Ormonde trundled a wheelbarrow; whoever will may see another noble lord faithfully depicted struggling with the first turf of a new line, while his tenantry look on and applaud. King Rail is to bring in the golden year. This is the triumph of peace, of industry; there shall be no more conquest or war. All the world shall (metaphorically) shake hands with each other out of first-class carriage windows. King Rail is the great leveller, the great peace-maker, and, above all, the great money-maker. The earth shall be turned into a huge iron spider's web, and we will all be spiders—even the flies.

Already, many persons' heads began to be a little turned by so much prosperity—to be had, too, for the signing of one's name in some cases, and in all for the payment of such ridiculously small sums that, from the crossing-sweepers upwards, everybody was a railway shareholder. Sir John Overton (having sold a corner of waste land near Overton for a sum large enough to gild every blade of grass which grew on it) had cast prejudice to the wind and become a director of the Cloppingford Junction Railway, and had had a quarrel in consequence with his old friend Sibthorpe. Sir Saville Fidelle, too, had lent the weight of his name to the company, of which it was understood that Mr. Hudson would be chairman.

Sir Saville had apparently come to the conclusion that the construction of railroads was no more derogatory to an English baronet than the making of the Foss-way to a Roman proprætor. He took an active part at the meetings of the board, and had decided opinions on the great gauge question. He was not yet in Parliament; but he had been heard to say that to be a railway director was much the same thing. Sir Saville's newly developed activity brought him a good deal in contact with Vincent, whom, however, except in his function of secretary, he habitually ignored in a manner very irritating to Amelia. When Sir Saville called upon his wife's sister, which he did occasionally, he always treated Vincent as if he were an acquaintance paying a morning call. He never asked for him, though he probably seldom or never called in Bloomsbury Square wholly on Amelia's account; but when Vincent came into the room would say, "How do? Heard anything more since the last meeting?"

"Sir Saville is the most detestable man I ever saw in my life!" exclaimed Amelia after one of these visits, in which Sir Saville had found an opportunity of asking one of these questions. "I wonder you put up with it, Richard! No one would think you were the master of the house to see the way he behaves."

"Sir Saville certainly has the talent of overlooking one's presence," said Vincent. His eyes were a little divided in their aim. Amelia had learned to understand this sign. "I wonder you put up with it, Richard!" she said. "If you take no notice, he will think you are afraid of him—odious wretch!"

"Perhaps he may think only that I do not notice him," replied Vincent, smiling unconcernedly. "But to speak seriously, my dear Amelia, reflect for an instant on what I should gain by resenting Sir Saville's bad manners. I should convert a covert insult into an open one, and give him the triumph of knowing he had wounded me. I could call him out, 'tis true; but it has always seemed to me the height of folly to invite a man who has already injured you, to shoot you by way of reparation."

"Good Heavens! Richard, you would never fight a duel? You would break my heart if you did." Amelia began to cry.

"I certainly never shall, unless it should be a great deal better worth my while than Sir Saville can ever make it."

"Richard, I never know what you mean— you are so sarcastic."

"My dear girl, do not make yourself wretched for nothing. Sir Saville shall never shoot me, nor dispose of me in any other way without my own consent. I am much more likely to hurt him than he is to hurt me; you pay your husband a poor compliment, Amelia, in bidding him be afraid of Sir Saville."

"I know you are much cleverer, of course; but it is so dreadful to hear you talk about duels," said poor Amelia wiping her eyes.

Just about the same moment (of an October afternoon), the doctor and Sophia were being put into a fly by Caleb (who was to follow next morning with the bulk of the luggage), on their way to London, where Dr. Simpson had taken a furnished house in Montagu Place, in order to be close to the Museum. The travellers very nearly lost their train, owing to the doctor's discovery, when the fly had gone half a mile, that a portion of his notes essential to his prosecuting his work *en route* had been forgotten in the confusion of the final directions to Caleb. Sophia, who made it a rule to yield in all points concerning the doctor's literary labours, suffered the fly to turn back without a word; but happily the doctor had scarce got his head in at the window on one side, when Sophia, from the other, was aware of Caleb breathlessly shouting, "Hi! hi!" and waving a roll of papers. The flyman thought he was running over some one, and pulled up his horse so suddenly as to give the doctor a smart blow on the head, and to jolt a parcel of books off the seat on to his toes; but the sight of the missing manuscript made up for all, and luckily the doctor always insisted (it was a tradition of Mr. Bolland) on being a great deal too early.

At as near as possible the same time, too, as Vincent was delivering his opinion on duelling, Mr. Culpepper was walking up and down in A'Deane's lodging, protesting that he would have the satisfaction of a gentleman, that he would not submit tamely to such an insult, that he would send the fellow a note that instant, and that A'Deane should carry it.

"Where's a pen and ink?" cried the enraged Culpepper.

Mr. A'Deane produced an inkstand from behind a loaf of bread in his cupboard. But such disastrous effects resulted from Mr.

Culpepper's attempts to indite his cartel with the contents, that one of the landlady's children was ultimately sent to buy a penny bottle at the nearest shop—which happened to be next door.

"I think I shall call him Tomkins," said Culpepper, when the ink was brought. "Willoughby, indeed! He's no more Willoughby than I am."

Mr. Culpepper (who was the son of a respectable linen-draper, of the Baptist persuasion, in a country town) had no more knowledge of the forms proper to be observed in sending a challenge, than was to be gleaned from the novels of the period—a selection of which in all the last stages of extreme dilapidation occupied the shelf of Mr. A'Deane's cheffonier.

"There's a challenge in *The Rivals*," he said doubtfully (while A'Deane was extracting the cork of the ink-bottle by means of a broken pen-knife). "But that's of no use. Think I should find it in any of these books?—*The Talisman—Ayesha the Maid of Kars—The*

Obeah Man—*Female Quixote*—*Paul Clifford*—*Eugene Aram*—*Last of the Mohicans*—they don't sound likely."

"There's a duel in *The Bride of Lammermoor*," said A'Deane, coming to the rescue, ink-bottle in hand.

"I want a challenge—a duel's no good," said Culpepper, looking into one book after another—"*Maxwell*—*Thaddeus of Warsaw*——"

"Try *The Young Duke*—there might be one there," suggested A'Deane.

"Or, *Matilda, a Tale of the Day*—that's more likely," said Culpepper.

While Mr. Culpepper turns the leaves of *Matilda*, it may be proper to state that the object of his wrath was Mr. Tomkyns Willoughby, and the cause a long series of attentions paid by that gentleman to Miss Annesley, culminating that very morning in the lady's denial of herself to Culpepper, who with his own ears heard her send the message that she "was particularly engaged," and heard also Willoughby's insolent laugh as the parlour door closed.

Richard III. was still on, and was a great success for both Willoughby and the manager. Horace, who played *Richmond,* had restored a good deal which is usually left out in acting editions—indeed, an anonymous person who wrote a letter in the *Post* criticizing the play, maliciously said that Mr. Lancaster made *Richmond* a more prominent part than *Richard.* Mr. Culpepper darkly hinted that this person was Willoughby himself. But the theatre was filled night after night, and Horace began to be so sanguine that Kiddle felt bound to be more of a wet blanket than ever.

"He'll launch out, if I don't keep his spirits from running away with him," he said to his wife. "He thinks he's out of the wood for good and all, because the theatre has paid its expenses for a month."

Horace, however, had other reasons for his high spirits, which he had not thought fit to tell Kiddle. The *Portico* Theatre would shortly be again to let, and Horace was in treaty for it. The *Portico* was an unlucky theatre, in an unfashionable neighbourhood; but it was small, and as three lessees in succession had failed to make it pay (in burlesque), Horace—or rather Vincent acting on his behalf—hoped to get it on somewhat moderate terms. Meanwhile, he much desired to make a brilliant *finale* at Dockhampton, and the feud between Willoughby and Culpepper threatened to seriously interfere with this. Culpepper did not send his rival a challenge, after all. His literary researches disclosed the fact that, by the laws of honour, the party challenged has the right of naming the weapons, which Culpepper and A'Deane were convinced would in the present case be swords—Mr. Willoughby being an admirable fencer.

"He gets a practice every night in *Richard*," observed A'Deane, "and he'd run you through the body as sure as you stand there."

"Say, as sure as his name is Tomkins," said Culpepper gloomily, tossing aside his works of reference. "But he shall not escape me."

Mr. Hillyard's business frequently called him to London about this time, and he usually contrived to turn aside on his journey, and "look in on his cousin Lancaster." He was shown in to Adelaide one evening, while Horace was at the theatre. Adelaide was in the nursery, and sent word for him to come up.

"Well, my dear, so these are my great-nephews," said the drysalter, when he had kissed them all round, with the exception of Susan, whom he nudged in the waist-band. "They make me feel as though I ought to be an old man; but for my part, I think these sort o' youngsters make a man feel younger somehow instead of older. I tell my daughters I grow ten years younger every time there's a wedding in the family." Here Hillyard winked at Susan, who retired into a chest of drawers and was heard to giggle.

"I went to the Lowther Arcade, when I was up in London town," continued Hillyard. "London Streets are to be paved with gold in real earnest before very long, they say; so uncle Hillyard thought it wouldn't ruin him to go into some o' them smart shops, where there's such nice young women behind the counters, to tempt ye to buy. And now who'll guess what I've brought? That youngster's out of the game," here Hillyard pointed to the bundle of lace and cambric which Adelaide held on her knee; "but perhaps you could find a tongue, young man."

Little Horace, to whom this was addressed, replied, "Uc-cu-il-yar, uc-cu-il-yar," in a voice loud enough to wake twenty babies, and began to drum with his feet upon the floor.

"Hush, Horry!" said Adelaide. "You will make baby cry."

Horry put up his fat little finger.

"Ush-sh-sh!" he said, in a loud whisper, standing on tip-toe to command his uncle's ear. "Ush-sh-sh! Baby ky."

"He's a sensible little chap, Addy; I hope he'll be a comfort to you," said Hillyard. "Well, now, let's see what came out of the Lowther Arcade, up in London town."

Uncle Hillyard produced a large brown paper parcel, which, with his hat and umbrella, he had brought upstairs with him. The brown paper covered grey paper, and the grey paper finally gave up its treasure in the shape of an engine, and half-a-dozen railway carriages, first, second, and third-class, stokers and guards, all complete. Further, there was a line of rail, on which the carriages would run at a great rate.

"Well, my man, do you know what that is?" said Horry's benevolent uncle, when these marvels were fully displayed.

"Puff-puff, puff-puff!" says Horry, with intense delight, and beginning to stamp again. Suddenly he left off, and running to his baby brother, who still lay asleep on Adelaide's knee, he whispered, "Don't ky, baby —Zu sall see to-mowow;" and, returning, began to draw the mimic train along, with the slowness of an epicure over a dainty dish. He left off again presently, to offer two pursed-up little lips to his uncle, thus entirely conquering the good-natured drysalter.

"That's as nice a little fellow as ever I set eyes on, Addy," he said, when Adelaide had taken him downstairs, and ordered him some refreshment. "Horace must be uncommon proud of him. So thoughtful for his age too."

"Horace cannot see so much of the children as he would wish—their noise disturbs him. I have had to teach Horry to be very quiet when his papa is at home."

"I called on your mother when I was in town. Uncommon well she looks, to be sure. Doctor hard at work as usual. They've got a nice house—only just round the corner from your square—and your mother seems quite at home. That Mr. Wigglesman, or Wigglesbottom—I always forget his name, was there, and one of the curates from St.

Pancras, and Mrs. Vincent called. How Vincent is getting on, to be sure! McLasher says he can do pretty much what he likes in the way of getting a man made a director of a company. Vincent asked me if I would care to be on this branch line; but, I said no— I understood the drysalting, and that was enough for me, but I hadn't no objection to putting some o' my money in the line, for them to use as understand such matters. So he laughed, and said that 'ud do as well, and he's going to buy me some shares in it. By the way, Addy, I bought a few for Horry and the little one—Vincent said it was always being done—they'll be a nice nest-egg for them, against they come of age."

"How kind of you, uncle!" said Adelaide blushing, and with the tears in her eyes. " But ought you —— ?"

"My dear, shares are dirt cheap in that line just now. Vincent says they'll go up, and be worth treble as much, but just now they're about the cheapest things you can buy. I went up to town in the *Prince o' Wales*—the old coach, you know, Addy," continued the drysalter. "It was the last journey it was to make to London. The coaches 'll all go; they'll come to be curiosities in time, like St. Mary's Church. There's a many changes in this world. Here's railways; how astonished my poor mother would have been to see 'em! and your youngsters upstairs won't notice 'em by the time they're men. And for the matter o' that, my poor mother would have been just as much astonished to see me coming here to talk over theayter matters, as serious as if they was a part o' the drysalting business. A good woman she was, and sat under Mr. Thorpe a many years."

Horace brought Theodore in with him, and presently Charlotte came home; she had been spending the evening with a friend. There was a great deal of talk about many things. Hillyard asked Horace if he was quite set on going to London.

"For my part," he said, "I don't see as

why you should. You can act here as well as there, and have things pretty much your own way."

"In London, I should have them quite my own way," said Horace, with less courtesy than usual. "I have been much thwarted and annoyed of late. I feel that the loftier efforts of the artist are thrown away on a public which can recall an actor night after night for the most commonplace melodramatic effects."

"Well, cousin Lancaster, I don't understand what's good, and what's bad in acting, though, of course, I know what I like. But it seems to me that you can do your best here as well as you can in town, every bit. You're the manager; there's no one to haul you over the coals."

"Indeed, I'm not so sure of that. Kiddle opposes every suggestion I make, and Willoughby has the insolence to impugn to my face my departure from traditionary conventionality. He seems to think that the interpretations of commonplace tragedians—mostly very ignorant persons—are to be binding for ever. I told him that I claimed the right to go straight to the text, and find as much in it as Shakespeare himself did, and would never submit to be clipped and checked by the limits of mediocrity."

"But you hold the purse, cousin Lancaster; you've got the pull of him there. He can't starve you out. And Vincent's been telling me that you're in a fair way to double every shilling you've got."

"My efforts are thrown away," said Horace with unusual warmth. "My good friend Warrener means to serve me, but he has an absurd prejudice against any elaboration of a part. He as good as told me this morning that I was too much like Willoughby; and the public think I'm not enough like him."

"Well, cousin Lancaster, there's a deal of satisfaction in that, to my mind. When one chap says there's too much of a thing, and another says there's too little of it, I always think 'tis just about right. Any way, I've found it so in the drysalting, and I doubt it's much the same in all trades."

"Your sentiments do you honour, Mr. Hillyard. I will always remember them when criticism disturbs me," exclaimed Mr. Paston. "Our friend Lancaster is too sensitive. An artist must work out his idea against the whole world—what is the cackle of fools to him?"

"You speak of what you do not understand, Paston," said Horace hotly. "You have never yet tasted the bitterness of knowing that your genius is unappreciated. If you heard a vulgar comic air applauded to the echo, while your sonata fell dead——"

"I should be provoked, no doubt, but I should console myself by composing another sonata. The joy of the musician in creating his work is greater than any joy he can feel when the multitude applaud."

"You are very philosophical, Mr. Paston," said Charlotte. "And you must have a tolerable opinion of your own merits to be so indifferent to praise."

"I am not indifferent to all praise," cried Theodore, flinging up his head, with flushed face and shining eyes. "The praise of those who are worthy to praise is very dear to me. But if no one would ever praise my work, I should not cease working. Horace knows, though he speaks thus, that the work is better than the praise."

"I have felt it to be so by moments; but the desire for recognition comes back, and will not be denied. It is surely no crime to covet the approbation of one's fellows?" said Horace with emotion.

"It must come in time, Horace. You have done a great deal already; every one has to wait," said Adelaide.

"Old Nollins—he's quite bedridden now—sent his duty, and a queer sort of a message," said Hillyard. "'He's a fine man,' says old Nollins, when I told him I was coming to see you. 'You tell him not to let the other one act *Iago* with him, 'cos he'll spoil all.' Poor old Nollins! he's getting rather childish now; but what you say about this new man brought it to my mind."

"Mr. Paston," said Adelaide, "let us have some music. We are all dull enough. Give us your sonata. Horace will take the piano."

Theodore's sonata pleased Mr. Hillyard very much, and so did Horace's voice when he sang "The Wolf," and "Mad Tom," in the midst of which the door opened, and a small, white figure, after an instant's pause on the threshold, rushed headlong into Adelaide's arms with a prolonged howl.

"Why, Horry, what is the matter?" said Adelaide and Charlotte in a breath, while Horace exclaimed—

"It is really too bad, Adelaide, that Susan does not prevent our being disturbed in this way. Horry, cease crying at once, and let your mother take you back to bed."

Adelaide's questions extracted from Horry that he had thought it was the earthquake come again—an admission which elicited the fact that Susan had some time before taken him to see a travelling panorama of the Earthquake of Lisbon, and had bidden him not tell his mamma.

CHAPTER II.

*There's a nice house in Tottenham Court, they say,
Fit for a single gentleman's small play.*
     *Remonstratory Ode, from the Elephant at
     Exeter 'Change.*

HORACE was growing impatient. He saw himself becoming one of many respectable actors, instead of, as he had fondly dreamed, rising at once to the first rank. A slowly won triumph had few attractions for him—he almost despised it. Genius, he thought, had no dealings with plodding patience. Nor could he understand Theodore Paston's comparative indifference to applause. An artist who could be almost contented with the pleasure his work afforded himself, seemed to Horace to underrate the merits of his work, and to be sadly lacking in spirit. He felt that he looked down from the heights of public recognition on the patient drudge who was only impatient to work.

It was an unfortunate circumstance in every way that Horace had no material obstacles to contend with. The steps are steep which lead to the Temple of Fame; and it is easier for a camel to go through the needle's eye than it is for a coach-and-four to climb them. The highest genius is above circumstance, and can bear to have all or nothing in its favour; but Horace was not of this stuff. He had too many advantages. He had striven hard, but he had not "agonized." A slight stutter, or any other curable disadvantage, would have been of inestimable service to him. With all his efforts, he had never quite reached the point where effort is lost in impetus. He was enthusiastic; he believed himself to be far more fiery than Theodore, who rejoiced in spirit as he composed music which would be unheard and unknown for years. And it must be owned that there was much excuse for his impatient desire for fame. A poet, a painter, a musician, can appeal to posterity; an actor must triumph to-day, or never. His triumph is more visible than theirs for the moment, but it is necessarily concentrated into a lifetime; theirs may extend through the ages. Their works follow them; he leaves behind him only his name, and the tradition of a gesture or a frown.

The *Portico* offered an alluring prospect to Horace. He need not there spend time and money on mere vulgar spectacles, for which, indeed, its stage was scarcely large enough. Everything would be more within compass, and the manager need not be the slave of any one set of play-goers. The select few for whom the common run of pieces had no attractions, would be the fitting audience for the tragedies which Horace had written as much to prove himself an actor as a poet. In every line of the chief part in each of them he had, as he wrote it, heard his own voice declaiming, and seen the hand which held the pen lending majestic action to the words. He was *Camillus*, coming to Rome's gate, *inter pendendum aurum*, to hurl back in the teeth of the Gaul that *intoleranda Romanis vox;* and *Jugurtha*, turning on the steps of the Mammertine to cry, " Romans, your bath is cold ! " He stood, as *Roderick*, before the brazen giants, presumptuous and haughty; he knew the very angle at which he would fold his arms in his royal mantle, as he watched the Vision of the Future. There was not a detail in the development of the plots, nor a turn of speech in the parts destined for himself, which was not planned to display his own powers. It was no wonder that Kiddle, to whom two or three of the plays had been reluctantly submitted by their author, observed, in the privacy of his family, that he shouldn't have known *Jugurtha* from *Camillus*, if *Jugurtha* wasn't a blackamoor.

Mr. Willoughby had persevered in his attentions to Miss Annesley, who flirted with him in a manner calculated to drive the unfortunate Culpepper mad. Theodore Paston, who considered Willoughby an example of all that acting ought not to be, and to be further incapable of improvement, was becoming almost as impatient as Horace himself. To add to the dissensions prevailing in the company, Miss Annesley and Miss Elton were no longer friends. Miss Elton, who had a romantic admiration for the manager, and who was perhaps piqued at the airs her Annabella had assumed, on the strength of her new conquest, spoke her mind one day with some plainness. The people that paid one most compliments were not always the most worth having compliments from, said Miss Elton; and playing at a transpontine theatre did not make one a gentleman, nor an actor either—nor yet a judge of acting, for that matter. On Miss Annesley inquiring what Miss Elton meant by transpontine theatres, that young lady replied that she meant whatever anybody liked to think; and that she had always understood that transpontine actors were rather low than otherwise, though some people were so proud of being noticed by them, that they thought nobody else good enough to speak to. This retort brought about a very pretty quarrel between the two ladies. Miss Elton, who was usually a very gentle person, had been roused to this display of opinion and temper by a complication of motives, which might have been likened to the rowels of a spur, inasmuch as they were goads springing from a common centre—the London actor's overbearing insolence.

Miss Elton had the moral support of the entire company, with the sole exception of Miss Annesley, whose pretty little head was turned by Willoughby's assurances of the sensation she would make at *Lorrimers, Wells,* and whose vanity had long been piqued by Horace's insensibility to her merits. The manager had actually told her she was too vivacious and trivial! But then, as every one knew, he was eaten up with his own acting, and wanted to keep everybody else in the shade. He had done this with poor Mr. Culpepper—who grumbled, but always submitted; but Willoughby was not to be kept in the shade at Dockhampton, after having shone at *Lorrimers, Wells.*

But the worst was yet to come. On the afternoon of the day following Hillyard's arrival, Adelaide came home from a charitable visit to poor Larkin's sick wife (he had found his way back to Dockhampton some weeks before, in great distress, and begged to be taken on again, if it were but as a "super"), to find Horace furious, and Kiddle, Hillyard, and Charlotte endeavouring to calm him.

"Put up with it for a few weeks more, Horace," said Charlotte. "Don't leave the place in a huff!"

"Huff! It's maddening! It is destroying the purpose of my life—I have been tortured by miserable sordid details of one sort or other, ever since I took the theatre!" cried Horace, who stood by the mantel-piece, and paced up and down on the rug when he was not speaking.

"These kind of accidents will happen, Mr. Lancaster—every manager has to put up with 'em at one time or other, and worse too, sometimes. We've come off easy. We ain't had a fire, nor a staircase smashed. Now, if you was all burnt out, like poor Mr. Ducrow——"

Horace groaned.

"He went mad, poor man, didn't he?" said Hillyard. "S'pose he wasn't insured. I hope you are, cousin Lancaster? A theatre's a risky place, what with all the lights, and such a lot o' woodwork about, that 'ud go like touchwood."

"It's past three now," said Kiddle, "and if we're to put on *George Barnwell*——"

"I'll close the theatre at once; I am sick of pandering to a depraved taste!" and Horace flung down the *Post*, in which he had been reading his own advertisement.

"Now, now; don't be too hard, cousin

Lancaster!" said Hillyard. "The young lady's a saucy piece, I don't doubt; but she's uncommon pretty, and got a sparkling eye."

"Bless your heart, sir, Mr. Lancaster wasn't talking of Miss Annesley; he means the play. He set out with the intention of producing nothing but the legitimate, you know, sir; but I tell him, the public gets tired of the legitimate," said Kiddle in an appealing tone.

"I s'pose you mean Shakespeare by the legitimate? There's wonderful sensible things in him every now and then, to be sure—as good as a sermon every bit. I've often wished my poor mother could have read them. But perhaps, for plain folks, Shakespeare's rather hard reading—in parts——"

"That's just it, sir," said Kiddle eagerly. "The whole thing, as you've put it, lays in a nutshell. Now, in *George Barnwell*——"

"He was a 'prentice, as murdered his master, wasn't he?" said Hillyard. "I remember hearing an uncle o' mine—a pewterer he was, an' lived in Shoreditch—say the masters used to send their 'prentices to see *George Barnwell*, as a warning to 'em. A good moral piece, I've always heard was *George Barnwell*."

"We could surely put on *Hamlet?*" said Horace, who had paid not the slightest attention to this conversation.

"Not very well, with three of the principal parts *horse de combat*," said Kiddle, who felt himself fortified by Hillyard. "The lady's in hysterics, and as for the gentlemen, I don't know which of 'em's the worse to look at. And, as ill luck would have it," continued the hypocritical stage manager, "it was some o' the scenery in *Hamlet* as Willoughby went through. The castle of Elsinore, and some o' the palace is smashed, and it'll take two or three days to——"

"Have it your own way. Put on *George Barnwell*," said Horace, as sullenly as was possible to him.

"I s'pose I'd better get some handbills printed, just to say that, owing to the indisposition of two of the——"

"Damn it, sir! say what you please, and let me hear no more of the matter! I am disgusted!" And Horace left the room.

"He is put out, and no mistake," said Kiddle. "I never heard him swear before, that I remember. Perhaps if he swore a little oftener when he was angry, it 'ud be better for him, and make him more ready to hear reason. You'll pardon me, ladies; I'd forgot your presence for the moment. I must be off. Your servant, sir. Good afternoon, ladies."

As soon as Mr. Kiddle had shut the door, Adelaide begged for an explanation, and was told that the quarrel between Culpepper and Willoughby had broken out that morning at rehearsal; that Willoughby had made some slighting remark, and that Culpepper had struck him. There had been a fight, in which neither party had had much the better, although Willoughby had been temporarily discomfited, by falling against some scenery, which, being old and rotten, gave way, ignominiously entangling him in the canvas.

During the scuffle, words were interchanged as well as blows. Miss Annesley, who had not left the theatre, hearing the noise, ran shrieking to the spot, whereupon Culpepper pointing to the struggling Willoughby whose legs alone were visible at the moment, said calmly, "There is the gentleman, madam, in whose fate you show so deep an interest." "Villain!" cried Willoughby, extricating himself from the *débris*. "That lady is my wife. Insult her if you dare!"

"They wanted to be at each other again, then, it seems," said Hillyard, "but Kiddle and some more parted 'em, and a pretty row there must have been. Miss Annesley—or Mrs. Willoughby, I s'pose we ought to say—fainted, and Culpepper called Willoughby a traitor, and I don't know what all; and there was the devil to pay all round."

If anything had been wanting to complete Horace's disgust with his present position, this would have done it. He attributed all that had happened to his having been persuaded to depart from his principles, and descend to a lower level. He at once closed with the *Portico,* and only endured the necessary delay, because he could now see its limit.

CHAPTER III.

Thank your own wilful folly, that hath changed you
From an empress to a bondswoman.
The Emperor of the East.

IT is a great mistake to reckon too much on any one's stupidity or weakness. We had really better reckon on the good qualities he may possess; we shall, of course, be sometimes disappointed, but the disappointment is seldom as serious in its consequences as those which result from the other error. Many a well-planned conspiracy has been revealed by some person supposed too dull to perceive what was going on. Many a town has fallen, because the commandant underrated the ingenuity of the enemy. It is much safer to suppose that one's adversary is cleverer than one's self, or at least to act as if he were. To some, this may appear Machiavellian, if not immoral. But with a few exceptions (more apparent than real), the dishonest mind is incapable of anything so near akin to humility as this high estimation of others. It partakes of the essence of unselfishness to be able to put one's self in the place of another so completely that we can see the weak places of our own position. The dishonest man's fixed belief is that he is much cleverer than the honest man. Rogues are generally found out through their faith in mankind's folly.

But it is almost more fatal to reckon on weakness than on folly. Sir Saville Fidelle seemed to Blanche, and to most people, to have as near as possible no character at all. He was not clever, not brilliant, not industrious. He did nothing, and yet did not seem conspicuously idle. He did not appear particularly fond of amusements, he did not seek excitement—nor did he shun it. Whatever any one should have said of him would have seemed to need qualification. A capacity for sullen obstinacy was the only positive quality which people attributed to him, and obstinacy, as we all know, is only a strong *won't*. But Blanche Overton soon found that in marrying him she had reckoned entirely without her host. In civilized life we have but very little hold on any one who is absolutely indifferent to our opinions and feelings, and absolutely fixed in his own purposes. So indifferent and so fixed was Sir Saville, that, although Blanche was always trying to assert her will against his, he was by no means dissatisfied with his choice. She received his guests, and covered his own want of conversational powers; she was the pivot upon which his social life turned—and that was all he had ever desired of her. She gave him an importance he could never have had as a bachelor who was not a "ladies' man." Even since her father's accession of fortune she was considered to have made an advantageous match; but her connections were quite equal to his own, and Sir Saville often reflected that he could not have done better. Blanche was less contented. She had counted on a pliant, if not an indulgent husband, and her vanity was piqued by his disregard of her caprices.

Sir Saville had disappointed his wife's anticipations as to his future conduct in almost every way but one. He was jealous of Horace Lancaster. And hitherto his jealousy had been an unmixed annoyance. It had not even yielded Blanche any of the perfectly harmless excitement she had promised herself from a strictly platonic flirtation with her rejected suitor. She had never seen Mr. Lancaster since her marriage, but Sir Saville had not forgotten him. Sir Saville never lost his temper with his wife, but he had a way of dropping a sneering allusion to " player fellows," which cut her pride to the quick. It was so new a thing to the haughty Blanche to be the sneered-at, that surprise kept her silent at first, and afterwards pride whispered that an insulting insinuation is better unnoticed. Sir Saville, whose own pride was as intense as it was narrow, had accidentally learned that rumour had once connected the names of Horace Lancaster and Blanche Overton, and it galled him to think that the world might even then be whispering, "If she liked anybody, it was him, depend on it. A much finer man than Fidelle, you know." These words, which he had heard one man say to another at the club, haunted him perpetually. He was intensely conscious of the disadvantageous appearance he made in society, although he despised the social successes of others, and especially of Vincent. But there was a sting in the thought that his wife would have preferred a man of no birth whatever (for, to Sir Saville, an East India Director was a tradesman), and a far worse sting in the thought that the world knew it. Blanche, who understood her husband a little better by this time, was yet very much surprised when he said one morning at breakfast—

"That fellow Lancaster, that your mother used to have at her house, has taken the *Portico* Theatre. I fancy he couldn't make it pay at Dockhampton. We'll go and see him. I never thought the fellow could act— he'd be monstrous awkward on the stage, I should think—but he had impudence enough for anything. We'll patronize him, and please your mother—she's sure to take him up."

Now that Blanche was married, there was, of course, no reason why Lady Overton should not take up Horace as much as she pleased. In fact, as Vincent's friend, he had a positive claim on her. And she felt free to admit now that Mr. Lancaster was altogether a very delightful person, and quite an acquisition to one's visiting list. Sir John, who saw the re-opening of the *Portico* advertised, observed that a man had a right to please himself, of course, but, demmy, it was carrying it too far when a gentleman turned a common play actor—adding that it was a sad pity he ever took up with the idea, for, demmy if he didn't believe Blanche would have had him.

"My dear, for Heaven's sake don't be so indiscreet!" said Lady Overton.

"Indiscreet? Well, perhaps he is, but he's a better-looking chap than your handsome son-in-law, my lady. I don't mean Vincent," said Sir John, winking at Lina. "'Second Fiddle,' they used to call him, Gerald told me," continued Sir John chuckling; "but he don't play that with Blanche, or I'm much mistaken. Well, if I was a woman, demmy if I wouldn't sooner have had Lancaster, stage plays and all, than a sulky fool with white eyelashes, that can't say 'bo' to a goose."

Sir John and his son-in-law had served on the same board of railway directors, with the effect of changing the antipathy which the elder man had always felt for the younger, to a lively dislike. Since his illness, Sir John was more choleric than ever, and at even less pains to conceal his opinions.

Lady Fidelle, who generally knew her own mind remarkably well, passed the time between the announcement of Horace's appearance and the opening night in a state of very unpleasant indecision. She had returned Horace's passion just enough to dislike going with her husband to see him in a position of which she herself had been ashamed, and of which Sir Saville spoke with the most offensive contempt. She felt sure that Sir Saville wished to humiliate her, by compelling her to see the man she had almost loved, " playing the merry Andrew," as he coarsely put it. Sir Saville doubtless hoped that Horace would be unfavourably received. Blanche had a keen sense of the ludicrous, and remembered that she herself had often laughed at Horace's affectations. She did not anticipate a triumph for him, and she knew that his failure would be full of humiliation for her.

But when the day came, and Blanche pleaded a headache, Sir Saville looked at her critically, and said, " You are perfectly well, and it is my desire that you go. People know that the fellow used to visit at your mother's, and I don't choose your absence to be remarked. An interpretation might be put upon it which I will not endure."

When Sir Saville spoke like this, it was always better to yield. He knew how to make disobedience extremely disagreeable.

CHAPTER IV.

Julia. He plays false, father.
Host. How? out of time on the strings?
Julia. Not so; but yet so false that he grieves my very heart-strings.—*Two Gentlemen of Verona.*

IT was with something very like dismay that Adelaide saw Sir Saville and Lady Fidelle enter their box. Sir Saville seemed to Adelaide considerably changed since that dinner-party at the Overtons', which might have happened a hundred years ago, for the distance in thought and emotion which divided it from to-night; or only yesterday, for the vividness with which every incident came thronging back into her memory.

Sir Saville, who then had looked very much

like an imperfectly finished chalk sketch of a man, and in whose face Adelaide had been able to detect no possibilities of anything stronger than peevishness, had developed into an unpleasantly faithful resemblance to a ferret. His eyes seemed to have grown keener and quicker; his nose was sharper, and his face had quite lost that flabbiness over which Sir John and Gerald had once made merry. He looked elaborately and offensively bored; and Adelaide's cheeks flamed with wrath at the insolent use he made of his eye-glass. But the languid insolence of his whole manner could not hide from her that Sir Saville Fidelle had "something in him," after all, and something eminently disagreeable. Blanche's face had hardened in every line, and her mouth had a weary, discontented expression; there was defeat and yet defiance in her manner, as she watched the performance. Adelaide had perhaps never yet been torn by such a conflict of emotions as raged in her, while Horace reproached *Ophelia*, and Lady

Fidelle fanned herself, now fast, now slowly, with eyes which never wandered from Horace for a moment. Had he seen her? Adelaide thought she saw him start; but if he did, it was with some feeling very unlike those which were almost suffocating her. The light came into his eyes, and his voice grew richer than ever—it absolutely rang through the house, as he cried (seeming to look full at Lady Fidelle)—

"Ha, ha! Are you honest?"

Adelaide knew that it was highly unlikely Horace really saw Lady Fidelle, across the glare and bedazzlement of the foot-lights; but his eyes seemed to burn with a withering intensity which could scarcely be directed at vacancy, and he was certainly not looking at *Ophelia*. Adelaide's own eyes turned against her will to Lady Fidelle. She was sitting motionless, and was extremely pale; Adelaide thought she was going to faint. Sir Saville appeared to have observed her indisposition, for he whispered to her; but she only shook her head, not even turning towards him.

The house was full, and the audience sympathetic; and Horace, who had been for days in a nervous agony, had recovered complete self-possession. Again and again a round of applause followed the delivery of a telling passage, and Adelaide felt a certain fierce pleasure in the thought that Blanche was witnessing his triumph. How princely he looked to-night! And how mean and odious was Sir Saville! Adelaide's very heart seemed on fire. Pride at Horace's triumph before this haughty woman, indignation at the insolence of Sir Saville's air and attitude, jealousy of Horace's possible feelings, and the most agonizing desire to know what he and Blanche really felt—all these were as separate flames scorching her, until she could endure no more, and leant, half-fainting, against the side of her box, hidden by the curtain, which also hid from her the causes of her emotion. Adelaide was frightened at herself—to her gentle nature, the extreme intensity of the pain she felt seemed a sin. But she could not think— she could but feel that here was Blanche watching Horace with a defiant face, and Horace seeming to be playing to her only. What did Blanche feel? What did Horace feel? Did she repent? Did he? Adelaide's whole being shrank and shrivelled at the bare thought; and yet she was not jealous in the ordinary sense of the word. The fiery pain which wrung her heart as with physical agony was due to no thoughts which she harboured, then or ever. Adelaide thought nothing; she only saw, and heard, and felt. When the intolerable conflict of feeling allowed her to think, she was angry and ashamed at her own emotion. Horace had never, by word or deed, given her the slightest excuse for what she felt. She bitterly reproached herself for the pain she could not reason away. And yet it was the sight of Blanche, not that of Horace (although she believed him to be aware of

Lady Fidelle's presence), which tortured her. A strange idea oppressed her that Blanche had the first claim, and that Horace could not, if he would, ignore it, if Blanche still loved him.

And this was the night of Horace's triumph. He had looked forward to this for years, and now it had come, and she, who ought to have been rejoicing, was distracted by unworthy jealousy! She would have hidden herself—and shut out the causes of her pain—by the friendly shelter of the curtain; but she feared lest her mother or Charlotte should observe her emotion, so she steadily turned her face towards the stage. But she knew little of the progress of the play, though ever after she had a distinct impression of Horace, acting like one inspired, and towering majestic—the one real figure in the horrible nightmare which oppressed her.

"This is success at last," whispered Charlotte, slipping her hand into Adelaide's. "Why, Addy, you're faint! Take my fan, it's larger than yours. The heat is overpowering."

Whether or no Horace was playing to Lady Fidelle, he had certainly never before risen so high above the self-consciousness which generally marred his best efforts. Lady Fidelle so far forgot herself as to doubt for several minutes whether her position as Sir Saville's wife was after all so immeasurably more to be desired than her position would have been as the wife of Horace Lancaster. She, too, was torn by conflicting passions. Despite her position and her prospects, she felt that she had been worsted in the game of life, and worsted by a man whom she had despised. Comparing him now with Horace, she loathed him. He was a little flushed with wine, his small eyes glittered. She did not love Horace; love and pride are the two master-passions of human nature, and in Blanche, pride and not love had always been lord of all. But she had a heart, though a cold one; and it was capable of feeling some very keen pangs. Vexation, humiliation, and vain regret can prick a proud heart very sharply.

"Oh, Addy, don't you feel happy?" said Charlotte, when, after the fourth act, Horace was called for. Adelaide involuntarily glanced across the house just as Lady Fidelle sank back in her chair in a dead faint.

Horace was never in haste to disrobe, and on this first night, when every one was pressing round to congratulate him, he had but just entered his dressing-room, when there was a sharp knock at the door. "Come in!" said Horace, who was getting out of his doublet.

"I want to say something to you, and this is as good a place as any other," said the intruder, closing the door.

"Sir Saville Fidelle!" exclaimed Horace.

"I don't suppose you expected to see me," said Sir Saville, who kept his hat on his head, and whose manner it was impossible to mistake.

"I needn't mention names, but when a fellow like you dares to ogle a lady before a whole theatre, it's as well some one should let him know that though a gentleman can't demand satisfaction from him, he can horsewhip him!"

Sir Saville did not deliver this speech so glibly as it is here set down—wine taken upon an angry stomach is apt to get into the head, and Sir Saville's head was rather weak in this respect.

"I do not understand you, sir," said Horace. "This is an unwarrantable intrusion, and I am not disposed to take your insolence tamely."

"I dare say not. All this finery makes you forget who you are; but if you presume on former acquaintance to call on any lady——"

" Sir, you are not sober, and I therefore excuse you; otherwise, be assured——"

"Damn you! How dare you behave as you did to-night?" said Sir Saville, who had lost all control of himself.

"If you do not immediately quit this place, I shall have you removed by force," said Horace. "I am at a loss to know how you were allowed to pass."

"Never mind that," said Sir Saville, who was leaning against the door. "I want to make you clearly understand that if you presume on any acquaintance—with——"

"This is too much!" cried Horace. "Sir, quit this place instantly." He took Sir Saville by the collar, and forcibly removed him from the door.

The noise brought Theodore, and three or four others.

"Sir Saville Fidelle! What, in Heaven's name——?" began Theodore.

"I'll have satisfaction for this," said Sir Saville, making a great effort to sober himself, and speaking between his set teeth. "I've been publicly insulted by a vulgar upstart."

"This is my theatre, sir, and it is at your peril you stay here another instant! Show the gentleman out this instant, and never admit him again!" shouted Horace stamping his foot.

There was a difference of opinion as to the precise manner of Sir Saville's exit—Theodore inclining to think that he fell, and Mr. Culpepper that Horace flung him down the three or four steps leading in the desired direction. In either case, his exit was sufficiently ignominious, and he was not too drunk to retain a clear recollection of how he came by the numerous bruises he sustained.

"It is very disagreeable that this should have happened to-night," said Horace, as he left the theatre with Theodore.

"Vincent said he was haughty and ungracious; but I should not have thought that he would have condescended to such an exhibition of himself."

"He had been taking wine freely," said Horace. "Nothing should ever induce me to stoop to *that* degradation. In spite of my annoyance, his appearance was so ludicrous that I could have laughed. If you ever crave for a draught of Lethe, Theodore, let it not be *that*."

Adelaide could never decide whether pain or pleasure predominated in the excitement of that night. She was left in happy ignorance of what had occurred behind the scenes, and Horace forgot all but his triumph. Vincent (who had been finding Lady Overton's carriage while Sir Saville was bribing an attendant to show him the manager's dressing-room) was very well satisfied, but did not seem to think that a favourable reception was an infallible augury of permanent success.

"I must say, Mr. Vincent, you are a wet blanket!" cried Sophia.

"I want Horace to remember that nothing is done, while aught remains to do," said Vincent smiling.

Amidst the talking and laughing, the jokes of Mr. Meadows, who was in the most amazing spirits, the open exultation of Horace, Adelaide's eyes of unfathomable meaning, in which Charlotte read a thousand things (taught by her own heart to read her sister's eyes), Vincent's calm superiority to the excitement of the moment, Sophia's lively chatter, Theodore's suppressed excitement (which Charlotte knew rose in a higher wave than that which surged in the heart of Horace himself) —amidst all this, Charlotte stole away into the library. She wanted space and leisure to realize that the desire of Horace's life was accomplished; and the library seemed the fittest place whence to look back on the past. The spring evenings were chilly, and the fire had been kept in, but there was no other light. The room was dim and ghostly, and yet warm —the ghostliness was not awful. Charlotte stood by the fire and watched the light glimmer on the lettering of the books, and flicker on the ceiling, and thought, with no terror, that perhaps the unseen presence of her father's spirit made the room seem so full of habitation. Perhaps he came there still sometimes, and, unseen of them, saw what they did, and heard them speak. She hoped so. He would be glad to see Horace famous—honoured.

"Oh, Mr. Paston, how you frightened me!" said Charlotte, startled out of this reverie by his touch upon her arm.

"I beg your pardon; I had no idea you did not hear me," said Theodore, his hand still clasping her wrist. "You came here to think—and to rejoice. You have been weeping, but it is for joy more than for sorrow. Your brother's dream is fulfilled. Charlotte, will you ever rejoice for me as you do to-night for him? I, too, have hopes—ambitions—would my success be anything to you? I have waited a long time; I was too proud to ask, and you were too proud to listen. And yet I have fancied that you sometimes spared me a thought, and that you knew I was not so cold and philosophical as Horace thought me—that you knew me as eager as he—as full of hopes, of desire of fame."

"Yes, I knew," said Charlotte. "But you have courage to wait, and my poor Horace is so impatient."

"I am impatient, too, sometimes," said

Theodore. "You know it—you know me, and have always known me. Why would you never let me tell you I loved you? I have waited so long!"

"And so have I," said Charlotte, very low.

CHAPTER V.

Runs not this speech like iron through your blood?
Much Ado about Nothing.

THE weather has a great influence on some people, and perhaps the depression of spirits which Adelaide had felt for some days past was partly caused by the constant rain. It was now spring, but the young green of the trees showed pale and grey through the rainy mist, and every time she heard the trickle of accumulated rain-drops down the dripping window-panes, she thought of the dreary day when Horace's father was buried. In vain she tried to turn her thoughts to the pleasant subject of Charlotte's engagement to Theodore Paston. She had been hoping this would come about ever since the day when they wandered up and down the alleys at Hampton Court. The engagement lifted a weight off her own heart which she would never own even to herself that she carried, but which was there nevertheless. Adelaide was not one of those women who can think with complacency that their image will for ever occupy a heart in which they cannot reign themselves. But Theodore was connected very closely with the memory of the months immediately following old Mr. Lancaster's death, and as Adelaide thought of him and Charlotte, the funereal plumes seemed to nod again and the funereal gloom to settle down. Adelaide remembered herself—suddenly called into the tangle of life, not sure if she had any part in it or not, only knowing that in her cousin Horace she saw more than the realization of her girlish dreams of heroes of romance. Mr. Vincent, too—in those days he had wished to marry Charlotte. Charlotte doubted him, and was ashamed of her doubts. Adelaide had never been able to conquer her first feeling of constraint. She did not often think of the alteration of her uncle's will, but whenever she did, she felt an instant's pain as the question returned for the thousandth time, "Did he think she had influenced her uncle?" It was not in Adelaide's nature to be quickly suspicious; but she had grown up with a mother who had taught her how the world thinks, though she could not teach her to think as the world. This matter of a few thousand pounds, which Adelaide had never been conscious of possessing, lay like a barrier between Mr. Vincent and her thoughts of him. She would never feel quite free to judge him. She did not know that she disliked him. She was uneasy in his presence, and he himself had never grown familiar. But for those three thousand pounds, Adelaide would long ere now have overcome her reluctance to speak freely before him—his calm, inscrutable observation of her would have fallen harmless had she been sure that he did not despise her.

This was almost as unpleasant a subject as the one Adelaide had been trying to forget. But it was not much better when she busied herself in household matters. Everything she touched, every room she entered, reminded her afresh of that dreary day. In the dining-room, her uncle's portrait watched her from the wall. The library (where she had still many finishing touches to put to the arrangement of Horace's books) struck her with an intolerable sense of gloom. Horace's chair—the same in which his father died, had been moved to the other side of the table, so as to face the fireplace, above which now hung the picture of the famous Calliope. She seemed to smile down on Adelaide, as though she would have said, "I am safe enshrined here from wet and windy weather, and from time and varying fortunes, but you must fear them all."

The air seemed thick. Adelaide shivered, and made haste to finish her task. But upstairs in the drawing-room it was not much better. Painful thoughts which had not obtruded themselves for years now would not be exorcised. Her life at Bath Easton, her mother's hints and schemes after old Mr. Lancaster's death, the party at Lady Overton's —all these things rose up in her memory with strange distinctness. And with these came newer subjects for unwelcome thought.

The promise of Horace's first appearance had not been fulfilled—perhaps only the tremendous excitement of that night had lifted him for once out of himself, and above himself. He had relapsed a little since then. And he had expected to succeeded immediately in London. He blamed the audience, the critics; he would not listen to the most reasonable criticism. When Mr. Meadows told him that one great effort could never ensure success on the stage, whatever it might possibly do elsewhere, Horace retorted that a modern audience was incapable of recognizing a great effort. Adelaide was beginning to be seriously uneasy about him. She had for some time seen that he was restless and discontented; but lately he had looked haggard, and had given way to gloomy moods and fits of depression for which there seemed to be no sufficient cause. His melancholy after the death of his father was not like this. Adelaide feared that his health was suffering, although Horace impatiently denied it.

She was quite sure that he had confided more to Vincent than to herself; she had overheard Vincent saying something about the effect of some medicine, which she suspected Horace was taking under his direction. Mr. Meadows had asked him if he was well, and he had answered rather sharply that nothing was the matter with him but worry, at which Meadows had said, "Worry is like misfortune—it makes us acquainted with strange bedfellows," and had looked meaningly at Horace, or so Adelaide fancied. She was growing fanciful of late, and distrustful—distrustful of Vincent. Horace, who had so often said that he would risk no more than he could lose, had only that morning remarked that this was a very exceptional crisis, such as only occurred once in a hundred years, and that it would be folly not to take advantage of it—especially when so much might depend on his being able to defy public favour for a time.

Adelaide knew what this meant. An adverse criticism had appeared in one of the papers. It was very sarcastic in tone, but in substance it was only what Mr. Vincent had always said of Horace's acting—that it was too elaborate, that the effect of the whole was lost in the multitude of details, and that the actor never rose above an artificial passion.

"Gentlemen amateurs," said the critic, "have often ere this strutted and ranted their little day, and we should scarcely esteem Mr. Lancaster worthy of so much notice, were it not that he managed the Dockhampton Theatre with credit, and that his private fortune will probably keep him before the public somewhat longer than either his merits as an actor, or the grotesque resemblance to Shakespeare (upon which we understand he plumes himself), could possibly have done." Adelaide's cheeks flamed as she recalled this sentence. There was a little justice in the criticism, as even she was forced to admit; but yet it was most unjust, and most cruel! Horace had immensely improved—had not the *Post* (and Horace had a great respect for Mr. Warrener's opinion) said that he was on the right road, and was curing himself of his defects? It was only now and then that he fell back into the old way, and made one forget his part. On that first night at the *Portico* there had been nothing to complain of.

Adelaide told herself that the events of that first night had nothing to do with her depression of spirits. She knew now what had happened behind the scenes; by some means, a report had got into one of the papers—the same in which the criticism had appeared—and although no names were mentioned, it was impossible not to know who "the gentleman amateur, lately a provincial manager," was, who had "just become the lessee of a small theatre not a hundred miles from the Edmonton Road," and who, "it was reported, had had a *fracas* with an honourable baronet, not unknown in the railway world. A lady was said to be in the case."

Luckily for Adelaide's peace of mind, Horace had himself told her of the "*fracas*," before this impudent newspaper report appeared. It had made Horace very angry, and he had consulted with Vincent as to the possibility of demanding from the editor the name of his informant. Vincent thought this would only attract more attention, and do harm. The editor would almost certainly refuse to give his authority, and any explanation would make things worse. Mr. Vincent thought it not impossible that Sir Saville himself had inserted the paragraph—an idea rejected as preposterous by both Horace and Adelaide. Mr. Vincent, however, adhered to his opinion, pointing out that the word *fracas* was artfully chosen to give no idea of what had actually happened.

"The paragraph reads as though there had

been a dispute, and perhaps even a scuffle, in which neither party got much the worst," said Vincent, laying down the paper. "And the editor of the *Daily Express* is mixed up with the railroad movement, and knows Sir Saville; I have seen them together."

All this was exceedingly disagreeable, although Sir Saville had not sent Horace a challenge. He had said that he would horsewhip him, but Adelaide was not much more disturbed by this threat than was Horace himself. Pistols level inequalities, but Sir Saville armed with a cane would fare no better than on the night at the *Portico*. Several weeks had gone by, and no more had been heard of Sir Saville's horsewhip. Amelia Vincent, who detested him, had told Adelaide that he was more sulky than ever. Amelia also said he had had a quarrel with Blanche, who was in Paris, with Lady Overton and Lina, professedly on Gerald's account, who had just got an appointment in the Embassy.

Adelaide was in the nursery, beginning to

forget the dreary day, and all these unpleasant reflections, when the parlour-maid came to say that Mrs. Simpson was in the drawing-room, and would rather not come upstairs.

"There's a good little boy, and now run upstairs to nurse," said Sophia, after bestowing a hasty embrace on little Horace, who had begged to come down with his mother. He turned when he had opened the door.

"Are you going to scold mamma?" he asked in a doubtful voice.

"No, you silly boy. Bless me, what ideas the child gets into his head, Addy!"

Horry was not entirely wrong, however. Sophia had come to talk very seriously to her daughter. She had seen the criticism in the *Express*, and, which was worse, a prospectus of a new railroad, in the same paper, with Mr. Lancaster's name in the list of shareholders.

"And you did not know it, Addy?" said Sophia, carefully refolding her copy of the *Express*, and putting it into her reticule.

"I know that Horace has a great deal more

confidence in railway shares than he used to have; but we don't take the *Express*."

"And no more do I, and I shouldn't think of taking a paper that's entirely in the pay of the railway companies. I'm told that Vincent's hand-and-glove with the editor. Caleb showed me the paper. He's peculiar, but devoted to us, and he's got an idea that an enemy puts these things in—the other paragraph was in this paper. But that's not what I came about, annoying as it is. I always said it was a ridiculous thing for a man in Horace's position to go on the stage; but you have encouraged him in all his follies, Addy, and you'll rue it one day. You've spoiled your husband; you have no more influence over him than that child upstairs! But I do hope you'll take my advice now."

Sophia's advice was that if Horace did "meddle in railroads," he should at least act for himself. There was some excuse for Vincent's being his man of business while he was at Dockhampton, but now there was no reason whatever why he should leave things to him or any one else. "Besides," added Sophia, "it will very likely wean him from the theatre —they say railroad business is very exciting when you understand it. And it's a stepping-stone to Parliament now. They say Hudson could get into Parliament any day. He is evidently an extraordinarily clever man; and why on earth should not Horace go straight to him, instead of making Vincent his go-between?"

Adelaide quite agreed that this would be a good thing, if Horace would do it. But he did not like business, and he was so used to let Mr. Vincent manage for him.

"Yes," said Sophia, with much energy; "and it is Mr. Vincent's cue to keep him amused with his theatre, so that he never may like business. If Vincent had not made everything so easy for him, Horace would have given up this whim. Vincent, I am certain, does not believe Horace will ever become a great actor. Vincent is a clever man, much too clever not to see that Horace is not as clever as he thinks he is. It's of no use for you to be angry, Addy. I know good acting when I see it; and I know that somehow Horace never lets you forget he is acting— the *Express* says so in those very words. And Vincent knows it, and if he were Horace's friend, he would have used his influence to get him to give it up. Parliament is Horace's sphere; but you've no idea how to manage him. You never have an opinion—— "

" Yes, I have, mamma. I have told Horace that, now we are in London, I wish he would not leave things so entirely to Mr. Vincent. I thought he ought at least to know what was being done with his money."

" And what did he say ? "

" He said that he did know, and that Vincent understood these things so much better—— "

" That's true, I'll be bound. But there's never the least use in talking to a man as you talk to Horace. You approach the subject too openly. You don't watch your opportunity to slip in a hint, or make a suggestion. You don't like Vincent—Horace told me himself you did not, and he laid it to me—but you have never tried to undermine his influence in a quiet way, as a woman can. A woman can do anything with a man, if she knows how to set about it, and keeps on long enough."

"Mr. Vincent always seems to me to be very cold, but he has done a great deal for Horace——"

"For himself, you mean, Addy! Horace has been the making of him," said Sophia. "Well, child, you know what I think. *I* have done *my* part. I have never lost an opportunity of dropping a hint—and, though you won't believe it, a judicious hint is the best way to bring a man to hear reason, and it's all the better if he does not know how much you mean by it. But you are just like a child—you blurt out everything. Why, if I had been you, I'd have wormed some of Vincent's secrets out of him by this time."

"Mamma," said Adelaide, flushing with anger, "I do not want to be disrespectful to you, but such ways are underhand, and I shall never try them. Whatever I do, I shall do openly."

"And be a fool to the last!" said Sophia, thoroughly angry in her turn. "I wash my hands of you. Underhand, indeed! You would not be where you are now if I had left you to your openness! Horace would have gone on pining for Blanche till doomsday if I had not dropped a gentle hint——"

"Mamma! What do you mean?" said Adelaide in a hoarse, frightened voice.

Sophia saw she had gone too far. "I mean that I opened Horace's eyes to see his own happiness—and I'm sure he's dotingly fond of you—no one can doubt that—quite like a lover, I'm sure, even now, if he wasn't so absent sometimes. Addy, don't look so, child! Many a man needs a gentle hint to bring him to the point. I'm sure Horace was desperately in love with you, and with all his faults, I will say he has been a very indulgent husband. You've had nothing to complain of?"

"No, indeed, mamma."

"You must keep up your spirits, Addy—it's important in your condition. Now don't be ridiculous. A married woman has no business to be sentimental. Horace has got over his fancy for Blanche long ago, and you could twist him round your little finger if you liked. By-the-bye, they say Sir Saville Fidelle is very ill. Of course everybody knows who that paragraph referred to."

Adelaide sat perfectly still, after her mother left her. She had an indistinct recollection of rousing herself to say "good-bye," and of hearing the door close, but all clear memory stopped short at those terrible words, "You would not be where you are now, if I had left you to your openness!" Like a lightning flash there came the memory of the day when Horace first spoke to her of love—of his grave, changed looks, changed manner. He pitied her—she understood it now. He had never loved her—never loved any but Blanche, who fainted at the sight of him. She, and not adverse criticism, had so troubled his spirits, and made him so gloomy and irritable. This, too, was why his acting had been so laboured and artificial. He had said that Blanche was nothing to him—but he said it out of pity. Perhaps he believed it then—till he saw her. There was a Spanish mahogany cheffonier, with yellow satin fluted on the cupboard doors, and a long looking-glass above. Adelaide could see herself in it as she sat. Was Blanche so much more beautiful? Adelaide remembered the hard lines of her face, the jet-black hair, and the white brow—she was very handsome; but Adelaide thought that her own face looked softer and younger. What of that? What of anything, if Horace only pitied her? Poor Horace! Adelaide felt that it was cruel of Blanche to have brought this about. Perhaps the something which people said was wanting to make Horace really succeed, would have come if he had married her. "You would never have been where you are—— !"

Adelaide still sat there, long after it was quite dark, and the lamps were lighted in the Square. It did not seem a very long time, and yet she did not think much—she only heard those words constantly repeated, "You would never have been where you are—— !" Horace had lunched at Vincent's, and would not return till after the evening performance at the *Portico*. Charlotte was with Lina. Adelaide was quite alone. Once she heard a door open upstairs, and Horry's voice saying, "Let me go to mamma!"

CHAPTER VI.

Iago. Reputation is an idle and most false imposition; oft got without merit, and lost without deserving : you have lost no reputation at all, unless you repute yourself such a loser.

HORACE was in a bitter mood that day. The talk at luncheon turned chiefly on the comparative prospects of the companies with which Vincent had to do; but Horace would break in on Vincent's account of the several lines of route, the probable expense of working, and the traffic which might be reckoned upon, with wholly irrelevant abuse of Englishmen in general, as incapable of any but these sordid interests.

"The country is moved like one man by the

hope of making money; and, when it is made, nothing better will come of it than an outburst of vulgar display!" he exclaimed, as Vincent remarked that, on the lowest computation, shareholders might be certain of ten per cent. in the worst of the lines proposed. "What are we? A nation of stock-jobbers. Betting is the sole outlet for our romance—we are ashamed of poetry, but we can grow almost poetical over horse-racing."

"Nay, you must own that art is patronized at Court," said Vincent.

"In a manner which dishonours patrons and patronized. There is scarce a Court in Europe which has not at one time or other encouraged the arts in a manner which puts our ungenerous, unprincely barbarism to shame. It is only in England that an artist and a juggler are on the same level."

"Oh, Mr. Lancaster, how can you say so?" said Amelia.

"I could give a thousand instances, but one is enough. The son of an Icelandic woodcarver was carried to his grave in Copenhagen the other day, with princes for chief mourners. The way was strewn with sand and juniper leaves, as they used to do for the heroes of old —the king himself received the corpse at the church door—a whole nation mourned him. And at this very time, this man's statue of Byron—a masterpiece—is lying in the lumber-rooms at the Custom House; the Dean and Chapter object to its being placed in the Abbey."

"But Byron was a very wicked man, was he not? Perhaps that is why they object," said Amelia.

"They could have pardoned worse crimes in a general, or even an under-secretary. And to make the contrast more complete, while the King of Denmark stood by Thorwaldsen's grave, in England the people were all running to see Tom Thumb!—a creature whose sole merit is that he is the smallest of men," here Horace threw into his voice all the bitterness he was capable of; "was sent for to Buckingham Palace! A monstrosity! whose existence ought to be considered a misfortune——"

"Oh, Mr. Lancaster, they say he is perfectly well-made, and has such *charming* manners," cried Amelia. "And, really, I'm quite shocked to hear you say such disloyal things!"

"No man is more loyal than I am," said Horace. "But I ask you, Dick, whether a King of England ever paid such honour to a subject as was shown to Thorwaldsen by his King?"

"I am not a great student of history, and I cannot tell," said Vincent. "But it is possible that the King of Denmark reflected that the world would hardly have heard of Denmark of late years but for Thorwaldsen. Englishmen are not dependent upon artists for fame."

"Dick, you're a philosopher, not an artist."

"I am a prosaic person, I admit," said Vincent smiling. "Amelia, you will excuse us. We have some business to talk over."

Horace was doubly impatient to make himself a name, because he had resolved to bring out *Camillus*. He himself preferred his *Jugurtha*, but Kiddle made so strong an appeal against "beginning with a blackamoor," at which he was certain the audience would laugh, that Horace yielded. Of the original company, only Miss Elton, Mr. Culpepper, Larkin, and the stage manager had followed Horace to London. The luckless Larkin, who had knocked about the provinces ever since his dismissal, had signed the pledge, and fervently promised reformation.

Horace left Dockhampton amidst many "expressions of esteem and respect," to quote the *Post's* account of a dinner given to Mr. Lancaster, on the occasion of his retiring from the management of the theatre. A piece of plate was presented to him, with a suitable inscription, which commemorated his efforts to " elevate the drama." The *Post* observed that it was perhaps to be regretted that Mr. Lancaster had not remained in a town where the longer he was known the more he must be respected, and where, in the long run, his efforts could not fail to refine the public taste. Still, the *Post* admitted that Mr. Lancaster had not been supported as he ought to have been, and that a gentleman of education and fortune might well desire a wider sphere than even their town, flourishing and important as it was, could secure him.

Adelaide was looking very ill, but she would not own to feeling so. "She was very tired; the bustle of moving, and all the excitement, had been a little too much for her."

"You never found things too much for you before, Addy," said Charlotte, who was puzzled by her manner.

"Ah, poor dear! she'll have to be worse before's she's better," said Mrs. Staples, when Charlotte mentioned her anxiety.

Even Horace, who was now always shut up in the library, when he was not at the theatre, was struck by her altered looks. But it never occurred to any one that she was unhappy—

except, perhaps, about the unfriendly criticisms which appeared every now and then—in fact, as often as Horace played in a new character.

CHAPTER VII.

*So will it fare with Claudio:
When he shall hear she died upon his words,
The idea of her life shall sweetly creep
Into his study of imagination.*
      Much Ado about Nothing.

"The poor girl has got something on her mind," said Mr. Meadows. "The only chance is to find out what it is."

"I most solemnly assure you, that—beyond some annoyances of my own, quite insufficient to produce such an effect—I know of absolutely nothing," said Horace, walking up and down the dining-room in the greatest agitation. "She has been very silent for weeks past; she seemed to wish to be alone, but I attributed it to her condition."

"Her condition had nothing to do with it.

She has been brooding over something. Mrs. Simpson, as her mother, you should know her best. Have you no idea that anything may have occurred to annoy her? What did she mean by asking you why you said something?"

"I'm sure," faltered Sophia, "I never meant—she could not be so foolish—and I explained—there was positively nothing in it. I was a little annoyed, and said so, but we parted as good friends as ever."

"Sophia, for God's sake speak plainly!" said Horace. "Adelaide's life may depend on our knowing how to soothe her. Have you said anything?"

"It is very cruel of you to have so little regard for my feelings as a mother!" said Sophia, bursting into tears. "The poor darling is light-headed—she does not know what she says. And it was weeks ago, and we made it up in five minutes."

"What did you say, Sophia?" cried Horace angrily.

"It is so foolish, so unkind to throw the blame of Addy's illness upon me!" sobbed Sophia, who really did not believe that Adelaide could have taken certain words of hers so much to heart. "If you *will* make me speak, I wanted Addy to use her influence with you, to get you not to leave all your affairs to other people's management. There was no harm in that. I spoke only for your good. And Addy was so lukewarm about it, that I was vexed, and spoke hastily; but we made it up directly. And I'm sure Addy would never break her heart for a cross word from her mother."

"Don't afflict yourself, Mrs. Simpson, unnecessarily," said Mr. Meadows, touched by Sophia's distress. "If this was weeks ago, and you have been on friendly terms ever since, I don't see how it can have anything to do with it."

It was Mrs. Staples who had first started the idea that Adelaide had something on her mind. That experienced woman declared that she had thought so all along, "ever since Mrs. Lancaster began to mope." The nurse, who was a stranger, rather snubbed Mrs. Staples for "taking up with fancies;" but that good woman was not to be put down. She insisted upon it that there was "something on her mind," and that "if it could not be got off her mind, there was no saying what might happen," and this opinion she communicated to Mr. Meadows. He had been rather anxious from the first. Adelaide was feverish and strange. She burst into convulsive weeping when she was told that the child was a girl, and again when it was put into her arms. But though her mind wandered a little, she was tolerably quiet until her mother entered the room. The moment Sophia spoke, Adelaide began to moan and wail, and implore her to go away.

"Go away, mamma; go away! Why did you do it? Why did you tell me? I was so happy till I knew!" Then she would appeal to Horace, and entreat him to believe that she did not know. "But they said he was ill," she muttered to herself; "and perhaps he will die, and I shall die, and it will be all right at last."

When Horace spoke to her, she moaned and wept; but the presence of Sophia seemed to excite her to frenzy, and the nurse turned them both out of the room.

"You mark my words, it's something as Mrs. Simpson has said to her about money matters," said Mrs. Staples to Caleb, whom the doctor sent every hour to make inquiries. "It's my full belief Mr. Horace is a-ruining himself over his theatre, and she knows it, poor dear! Mrs. Simpson told her. I heard her a-saying so. *She* won't believe it could have took such effect on her mind; but it 'ud be a dreadful thing for Mr. Horace to have to work for his living; and he never used to do nothing, except just when he felt inclined."

Caleb repeated this conversation to his master, who listened very attentively. Full five minutes after Caleb had respectfully closed the study door, the doctor rose from his seat, paced up and down once or twice, with his hands behind him, and finally rang his bell.

"Caleb," said the doctor, "where is your mistress?"

"She's round in the Square, sir," replied Caleb, with a jerk of his head in that direction. "She couldn't abear to leave the house, though they say Mrs. Lancaster don't know her, and screeches out when she comes near."

The doctor uttered some inarticulate sounds as Caleb said this, and grew very red in the face.

"He went straight out, and took his hat, and he was a-crying like a child," said Caleb, in narrating the incident to Mrs. Staples.

"Mrs. Lancaster is much the same, sir, and don't know anybody, and Miss Charlotte is with her, and Mr. Horace is gone for another doctor, I believe, and Mrs. Simpson is in the dining-room," said Mrs. Staples in answer to Dr. Simpson's inquiries.

"I will speak to Mrs. Simpson, if you will allow me," he said.

Sophia, who had been crying, got up from the sofa as her husband came in. "They are going to have another opinion——" she began.

But the doctor waved his hand. "Sophia," he said, "what did you tell Adelaide about Horace?"

"Nothing," said Sophia, frightened at the doctor's manner. "That is nothing much—nothing—it is very cruel of Addy to make such a fuss about a word!" Sophia was trembling from head to foot, and presented a pitiable spectacle.

"Sophia," said the doctor gravely, "I insist upon knowing what you said to Adelaide about Horace, and which has preyed upon her mind."

"They are all in a league against me," sobbed Sophia. "This is Vincent's doing!"

"What did you say, Sophia?" persisted the doctor.

Bit by bit, Sophia at last confessed that she

had told Addy that Horace would never have married her had not a hint been given him that he had unconsciously won her affections.

"And was it so?" asked the doctor.

"I gave him a hint—he was going melancholy mad about that Miss Overton, who jilted him shamefully—and Addy liked him—and I'm sure he's very fond of her—I did no harm——"

"That is not the point, Sophia. The point is, did you lead Adelaide to suppose that her husband married her at your instance, and not from affection?"

"I told her Horace doted on her—I only said I gave him a hint—she provoked me so—I was sorry directly. You can't think I wished to hurt my own only child?" sobbed Sophia. "What if I did give him a hint? She's been married for years, and Horace is the best of husbands. That's what vexed me—seeing how fond he was of her, and how she let Vincent rule him. No one else would take a thing to heart that happened years ago. I'm sure I'm the most miserable woman in the world, and if Addy dies, I shall never be happy again! And you will hate me—I know how you dote on Addy."

"Nay, Sophia, I shall never hate you," said the doctor. "We have all much to be forgiven, but you have done very wrong, and only God can undo the consequences of your deed. Try to calm your mind, Sophia. His mercy is infinite; let us ask——" Here the doctor broke down, and saying abruptly, "Pray, Sophia, pray," he left the room.

Neither Sophia nor the doctor had heard a carriage draw up to the door—straw had been laid down that morning—and Dr. Simpson almost ran up against Horace in the hall. Mr. Meadows and another gentleman were just going upstairs.

"I must speak to you without delay," said Dr. Simpson, seizing Horace by the arm, and drawing him into the library.

The patient was in a highly excitable state,

with much fever. Danger? Well—here the great man hummed, and looked at Meadows—in these cases there was always more or less danger where there was fever. Get the prescription made up immediately. Keep the patient absolutely quiet. A natural sleep was the thing, of course—the nurse said she had not slept last night. Perfect quiet, and induce sleep by every possible means.

As soon as the great man had gone, Horace, who was painfully agitated, turned to Meadows.

"Would she know me?" he asked, hoarsely.

"My dear sir, you mustn't go near her. I won't answer for her life, if there's the least excitement."

"But I can disabuse her mind of a painful impression—I have just learned a circumstance——" Here Horace glanced towards Dr. Simpson, who had retired into the window. "She is under a delusion, which I can remove by a word."

"Well," said Meadows, "she is quieter just

now, and if you are certain you can set her mind at ease about anything—you know best whether it will tend to calm her mind. But you know the risk!"

* * * * *

"Adelaide," said Horace, kneeling down by her pillow and taking one of her hands in his, "try to listen to me a moment. My darling, what your mother said to me only roused me from an empty dream. I loved you when I first spoke to you of love—you only—and I have always loved you, my darling, my queen—I have longed too much for fame, and now God punishes me!"

"Horace, dear Horace, don't cry! I thought you pitied me," said Adelaide a little wildly. "I thought—oh, Horace, I have been so unhappy!"

"She is nothing to me; she is less than nothing," said Horace, passionately denying his old passion. "And you are everything!"

CHAPTER VIII.

Sibylla's golden bough, the great Elixir.
The City Madam.

THE most important constitutional changes nowadays do not cause half the commotion which was raised by "the Railway Plunder Bill," as the companies called it—and half England belonged to the companies, in one way or other. The House of Commons was deluged with petitions setting forth the wrongs of third-class passengers — how they were carried in trucks scarcely fit for cattle, and open to the weather; how the trains conveying them had orders to be as slow as they could, and as inconvenient in their hours of starting. At the same time, even the slowest locomotive moved fast enough to make it a serious matter that the cars were open to the winds. Poor working-people and their families arrived from a journey wet, miserable, and degraded—for the primæval third-class carriages were ingeniously contrived to express to the dullest eye how railway companies estimated their third-class passengers. The companies only want to wring out as much money as they can; the health and comfort of the passengers are nothing to them, say "your petitioners," and add that now we have no choice—go by rail we must, for the coaches are everywhere being taken off, and we are at the mercy of the railway directors.

On the other hand, the directors and shareholders besieged Sir Robert Peel and Mr. Gladstone with deputations, who argued, persuaded, entreated; but in vain. The Government stuck to its Bill, in spite of meetings and speeches, in which outraged directors raved about the "icy hand of power clutching the public works of the country." This figure was a little unfortunate, for the third-class petitioners had bitterly complained of having to travel in open trucks in snowy weather. Chairmen of opposing companies, who were working against each other tooth and nail, met in the same room to agree in denouncing this attempt to "bring our railways under the paws of Government." Government had touched more sore points than one— not only were decent means of carriage to be provided for all passengers, of whatever class, but certain provisions were made by the Bill for giving tremendous powers to the Board of Trade. After fifteen years, under certain conditions, the Board could reduce any railway's profits to ten per cent., and could do a great many other things, highly obnoxious to enterprising projectors and shareholders, who, knowing that they were going to revolutionize the whole traffic of the country, thought it monstrous they should not have everything their own way. Every town had its meetings, its petitions, its deputations to Ministers. The representatives of twenty-nine companies, with £50,000,000 to back them, talked themselves hoarse in a vain endeavour to persuade Peel and Gladstone that the Bill was against the spirit of English commerce. Glyn, Russell, and Hudson himself exhausted their eloquence on the Ministers—this was no mere demonstration, with speech and reply neatly written out and tied up with red tape the day before, but a genuine attempt to talk Ministers out of their Bill. Pamphlets flew in all directions. Members were plagued by directors, and threatened by their constituents. The directors were all agreed that it would ruin them to be compelled to carry their third-class passengers like Christians. Sir Robert, from his place in the House, requested that Government might be allowed to speak, and warned the country against a monopoly which would not even listen to an explanation. Mr. Gladstone said that "he would no more trust the railway proprietors on railway matters, than he would Gracchus speaking of sedition;" and the

Bishops were strong against Sunday travelling —especially for third-class passengers. But, although the Bill was not abandoned, Government was really beaten—so much was modified, and so much conceded.

And then the fever set in in good earnest. Never since the South Sea Bubble was there such a universal spirit of gambling. The fishers in the sea of speculation could not cast their nets quick enough to catch the fish which, both small and great, came praying to be caught. There was every variety of scheme, and every shade of dishonesty—from the merely over-sanguine company, which hoped to make good its liabilities, to the out-and-out swindlers, who got up a sham prospectus, with sham names, a sham capital, sham accounts, reports of meetings which were never held, and a sham map, where waste lands appeared as flourishing and populous districts, and towns were planted instead of peat-moss.

The railways had newspapers of their own; there were *Railway Globes, Worlds, Ex-*

presses, Examiners, Telegraphs, Standards, Shareholders' Advocates, Directors' Registers, Reviews. The *Iron Times* charged fabulous prices for advertisements inserted just after the leading article. All other newspapers were inflated to twice and thrice their natural size with advertisements — and herein were a symbol of the times they chronicled. "Double-doubles" did not suffice to contain the projects which sprang up like mushrooms in a night — drawn up by three or four adventurers in a dingy garret, but looking on paper every whit as solid as the prospectus of the Great Northern or Great Western Railway itself. Printers and lithographers could not work fast enough. Some men were concerned in as many as a hundred lines. The civil engineer was the man of the time. George Stephenson, who had been laughed at as a madman, pitied as a fool, and called a braggart, for saying he could make a steam-engine go twelve miles an hour, was now a very railway god. His name was sufficient to float a company. A few years ago, the idea of an engine which should go twelve miles an hour had been too much for faith to swallow; and now no engineering project was too daring. The public was ready to believe that engines could climb hills as easily as flies can walk on ceilings. There were to be pneumatic railways; railways in the streets of London, or carried on bridges overhead; while in the country the engines were to employ their surplus power in impregnating the earth with gases, and so make the very corn grow at railway speed.

No one was too high, no one was too low, to take a ticket in the vast lottery. From peers of the realm down to their own scullions and knife-boys, every one put a finger into the great railway *hazarde de la fourchette*. Respectable widows and spinsters took their hundreds out of the Bank and bought shares. The most cautious took the infection at last— it was impossible to see men making fortunes in a day, and not long for a share in the good luck which was actually going a-begging. And it was small wonder that the thoughtless and ignorant crowd rushed in as shareholders where the most sober and wary of men— directors of old-established insurance offices, and bankers of long standing, lent their names as committee men. One company was said to be able to command the votes of a hundred Members of Parliament. Members hawked about their vote and interest among opposing companies, just as their own constituents had done at their election. A company would buy a newspaper, and put in an editor who was a mere mouthpiece, and who would puff the company's projects, and run down all opposing ones. And of this stupendous and complicated movement, Hudson was the guiding spirit. He was connected, or believed to be connected, with most of the projects—he influenced them all. He was a man of no great education; his father was a farmer, and he himself was apprenticed at sixteen to a linen-draper in a second-rate street of York. His manners were so rough and peremptory that he offended the customers; he was clownish and even vulgar. But he was so energetic that his employer offered him a share in the business rather than lose him. At twenty-seven, Hudson was an enterprising linen-draper; then some money was left him. At thirty two, he was Lord Mayor of York, chief director of the York Union Banking Company, and the mainspring of the York and North Midland Railway. He was like one of his own locomotives—uncouth and irresistible. He had words in plenty, but was no orator; he bore down interruption as he bore down opposition, by his loud voice and his indomitable will. Men trusted him because he never for one instant doubted himself. His prodigious energy grew with the tremendous demands upon it; his no less prodigious memory enabled him to dispense with account-books — which possibly might have also proved inconvenient. He was worshipped by all parties—Tories, Whigs, and Radicals. What are minor differences when we are going to make our fortunes? Later, he was reviled by all parties, who, as soon as they were ruined, perceived the wickedness of unsuccessful speculation. He cannot be absolved from responsibility. He must have known that a crash was inevitable; but it is probable that he himself was to a great extent carried along with the stream to which he had given impetus and direction.

Even Horace was affected by the excitement. His wrath with Sophia was so great, that he would have put more confidence in Vincent than ever had he followed his own impulse. But Adelaide had suggested that he had perhaps been mistaken in withdrawing so much as he had lately done from the invigorating interests of life.

"You have been too much shut up to one set of thoughts," she said. "It has been so all your life—you have always lived in a world that you made for yourself."

"And you think, dearest, that I should do

well to live in a world which other people have made for me?"

"Yes—for a time. Other people seem to make things more real."

"You may be right. And yet I have always cherished the thought that the artist dwelt apart—as a priest, in sacred solitude. He should step down from his cloud—there should be a sacred mystery enveloping him."

"But he must not always stay there," said Adelaide. "He speaks to men and women, and he must be able to sympathize with them. Genius which has always lived up in a cloud on a mountain makes us shiver. We are most moved by the man who understands us best. I think that genius ought to try to be as like and not as unlike the commonplace people as it can."

"Ah, you learned that from Theodore," said Horace. "I cannot agree with it. It is a low view of genius."

"I have thought it myself, Horace, indeed. I know what touches me most. I admire the genius you speak of, but it is a kind of beautiful statue, which is very handsome, but one could do without it, and we should be quite content to put it away in a gallery, where we do not often go. But the other kind of genius, we never want to put far away. We admire the other most—it is more striking——"

"I am glad you admit that."

"But we get tired of it sooner."

"You are as bad as Theodore," said Horace, but very good-humouredly. "The present age has lost those elevated ideas of art as a lofty, and perhaps unattainable, ideal. But I have determined to take your advice, at least in part. I have already told Vincent that I wish to be initiated into the mysteries he is so competent to explain."

This conversation took place at Twickenham, whither Adelaide had been removed as soon as she could bear the journey. In consequence of her illness Horace had closed his theatre earlier than usual, and had spent his leisure in preparing his plays for the press.

Theodore had waited a good while for Fortune, and now she seemed quite in a hurry to show him favour. Almost as soon as Charlotte had promised to rejoice in his success, the *Capellmeister* wrote to his son to say that the Grand-Duke had been graciously pleased last Sunday to make particular inquiries as to Theodore's doings and prospects. "I took the opportunity of informing his serene Highness," continued the *Herr Capellmeister* Paston, "that you had composed an opera, but that you had no hopes of getting it brought out at either of the London opera-houses (I did not tell him you had had it returned to you). The Duke was good enough to say he should like to look at it. If it is as good all through as the parts you showed me when you were last here, I think it's just possible we might do it at Vogelheimsburg. The Duke likes nothing better than to patronize a young composer, except to discover him. If you feel disposed to try and let him discover you——"

Charlotte, on hearing this, instantly declared that the Grand-Duke must and should discover Theodore, and that he must go himself to Vogelheimsburg, both because the Duke would be likely to feel more interest in the opera if he could talk to the composer about it, and because that invaluable manuscript must by no means be entrusted to the post.

Theodore admitted that this was true; but to leave Charlotte——

"Oh, nonsense!" cried Charlotte. "You can write very often, and you need not be long gone—not very long. Go with you? Goodness me, no! I've got nothing ready, and Addy's not well enough for the least bustle. Besides, you'll be much more interesting as a bachelor. No, wait till you come back, and then, in case the Duke doesn't bring out the opera, you'll have me to console you." Charlotte was smiling, but there were tears in her eyes as she said that Theodore would have her to console him.

"So if I come back with my opera under

my arm, as I went, you won't be ashamed of me?" said Theodore with a quiver in his voice.

"Do you think I was ashamed of Horace, when that abominable criticism came out in the *Express?*" says Charlotte proudly.

CHAPTER IX.

Hamlet. Sir, I lack advancement.

SOME people say that genius is never conceited; others are as sure that it always believes in itself. Perhaps both are in the right. There is something akin to unselfishness and modesty in the very creative faculty which brings with it a sense of triumph more keenly exquisite than any which mere conqueror ever felt, and is happier than Alexander, for genius need never fear there shall be no more worlds left to conquer. The man of real genius is at once the least personal, and the most intensely personal of men, and may be known by this sign. He triumphs in his work, but the joy of doing is better to him than the praise of having done; and most of the praise he receives teaches him only how little worth is praise.

Theodore had felt this while he was writing his opera; but he felt it more after the Grand-Duke had ordered it to be put into rehearsal. "I am glad—yes, I am delighted," he wrote to Charlotte; "that is, I should feel noon was turned to midnight if my work were now refused—if the Duke changed his mind, for instance, in favour of some other composer. But half my music is thrown away upon them, even here. The Duke suggested yesterday that I should change the *andantino*, in the third act, to a *moderato*, which would entirely change the character of the *aria*. And every one who is a year or two older than myself thinks he is qualified to suggest, or criticize, or, worse than all, pay me compliments which show that he has misunderstood my meaning from the first note to the last. The son of the English banker—a fellow whom you have met at my aunt's, and who thinks he is a connoisseur because he has been to two or three concerts at

Hanover Square—said to me to-day, 'I like all I've heard of your opera, Paston' (the fellow contrived to be admitted to a rehearsal). 'I think it very good indeed—'pon my word I don't say it to flatter you. I assure you I think it's quite a success.' 'The devil you do!' said I. I could not help it—I could have taken his criticisms with patience, but not his praise. I dare say they will think this a proof of my conceit. Let them. I have always felt that praise must be offered as delicately to a gentleman as money, or it becomes a deadly insult."

The production of his opera detained Theodore in Vogelheimsburg longer than he had anticipated; and Horace, always generous, would not hear of his engagement at the *Portico* interfering for a moment with his career as a composer. The second violin was conducting, and was fully equal to all the needs of the *Portico*. If, added Horace, he had met with more recognition, it might have been no injustice to Theodore to consider him a permanent part of the company; but, as it was, it would only add to his mortification to know that he was hiding Theodore's light under the bushel of the *Portico*.

Theodore however had done his best for his friend. He had composed musical interludes to *Camillus* and *Jugurtha*, and had written a very spirited *March of the Gauls*, and a massive *Roman March* to herald the respective entrances of *Brennus* and *Camillus*, besides several slighter compositions, also for the benefit of the *Portico* orchestra.

The tone of Horace's letters had caused Theodore much uneasiness, but had hardly prepared him for the change which he saw in him on his return. He came flushed with the success of his opera, which had more than satisfied the Duke, and had fairly transported the *Herr Capellmeister*; and eager to enjoy his triumph a second time in telling it all to Charlotte. But he found Horace worn and irritable to a degree which shocked him, as it had shocked Adelaide. After the re-opening of the theatre, she had, at Horace's urgent wish, remained with Charlotte at Twickenham, where Horace spent every Sunday. He had made the purer air his reason for this wish, but in reality he wanted to hide from Adelaide his ill success, and the effect it had upon himself. He was desirous of sparing her pain, and still more desirous of sparing his own vanity. He could not endure the thought that she should hear the very faint praise which greeted his efforts. All his hopes were now centered on the tragedies, on whose success he counted to atone for all former disappointments. He watched the career of other actors with jealous eyes; no one, not even Adelaide, ever guessed how much it cost him to speak as ungrudgingly as he did of Macready, or how he winced to hear of the success of *Antigone*. In his secret heart, Horace felt himself capable of intenser passion than the great tragedian, whom he forced himself to acknowledge as great, but to whom he hesitated to ascribe genius, in the highest sense of the word. A triumph such as his, won step by step by indomitable perseverance, would not have contented Horace. To him such success as this seemed to prove nothing save greater powers of endurance, opposition worn out, and perhaps rivals outlived. His own dreams were more dazzling; he would fain have taken the Temple of Fame by assault, and have won immortality by a stroke.

Vincent's exhortations to work and wait, and Theodore Paston's reminders of the many now known to fame who worked and waited through half a lifetime, could but sound flat and unprofitable to a man possessed with such ideas as these. He would match himself with Alexander, not with Fabius; and the discovery that he must be content to plod and drudge his way to glory, was a bitter disappointment.

Horace was unfortunately but too consistent in his contempt and dislike of drudgery. When he wrote, he lashed himself up to fever heat, and was afraid of nothing so much as giving himself time to cool. He courted perpetual inspiration; he would not recognize the greatness of the tremendous self-control which can carry out coolly and resolutely the ideas conceived in heat and passion. His refined taste had always revolted at the thought of stimulating imagination by vulgar means, and he had only occasionally had recourse to any other, until the advent of Willoughby, and the mortifications and annoyances which followed. Horace was fretted by the thought that he was growing commonplace and prosaic—even vulgarized; a little opium seemed to him to restore his self-respect. In the exaltation which it produced, he forgot the smart of wounded vanity, and abandoned himself to meditation on his unfinished tragedies, rejoicing to know that he could command poetic fervour at will. Vincent, who had considerable medical knowledge, had discovered that Horace was forming this habit, and had tried to persuade him to give it up. But he was soon convinced that Horace's peculiarly excitable temperament needed some harmless sedative, and he knew quite as well as most doctors, as he smilingly assured Horace, how to prescribe for him so as to ensure that the sedative should be harmless. The immediate effect of Mr. Vincent's prescription was to soothe and calm his patient, without, so far as could be perceived, any unpleasant effect whatever.

Horace assured Adelaide, who had been made uneasy by something she one day overheard him say to Vincent, that he was perfectly well, and was simply taking a little precaution to counteract the tremendous strain he found it to act constantly in trying parts like those he now almost always appeared in. Adelaide had spoken to Mr. Meadows, but Horace, in answer to one or two questions the doctor put, said that he was well enough in body, in a tone which shewed that he did not choose to say much about his health.

Meadows, who had suspected for some time that the palpitations Horace confessed to being troubled with occasionally, did not proceed from indigestion, told Adelaide to watch him carefully, and soothe him as much as possible. "I don't quite like the look of him, my dear," said the good old doctor; "the life he lives is too great a strain for any man. I was rejoiced when he engaged that man at Dockhampton—I hoped he would allow himself a little rest. He's afraid I shall say he ought to rest now. Vincent is the only man who can influence him; and Vincent always gives his advice in such a take-it-or-leave-it style, that Horace feels it's a point of honour not to take it."

The result of all this was to make Adelaide very uneasy. While she was brooding over those words of her mother's, she had seen another proof of Horace's revived interest in Blanche, in his own admission that of late he had been compelled to take something to quiet his nerves.

Now that Theodore had returned, she disburdened her anxieties to him. They were all three, Theodore, Charlotte, and herself, looking out of the window on the lawn. A heavy fog hid the river, and blotted the trees in the garden into mere silhouettes. It was but a little past noon, but the day was dark, and the fog was growing denser every moment.

"Every time he comes down, he seems more worn and ill," said Charlotte, when Adelaide had told Theodore what Meadows had said. "He thinks we don't know how much he feels those abominable criticisms in the *Express*, but I believe they have made him ill. At Dockhampton, if things did go wrong sometimes, there was always a civil word in the *Post*. Even when it found fault, it was always friendly and respectful; but the *Express* is most insolent. I wonder who does it!"

"Some newspaper hack, who gets an extra half-guinea for a cutting notice," said Theodore contemptuously. "Very likely the same man who tried to write down Macready, till he saw it was of no use."

"They are not like most of the other criticisms," said Charlotte. "Or perhaps we think so, because they are about Horace."

"I am very sorry that Horace condescended to notice them," said Adelaide. "His letter was very dignified, certainly; but I am sorry."

"Critics are generally beneath contempt," cried Theodore, remembering the son of the banker at Vogelheimsburg. "Horace is too impatient. If he would go steadily on, he must gain a respectable position in time. But until he has done so, it is a mistake to bring out *Camillus*."

"What a brute I must have seemed!" said Theodore, when he was alone with Charlotte; "the moment I had said it was a pity to bring out *Camillus* just yet, I could have hid my face for shame. And yet, believe me, Charlotte, I should have said it with my own opera still lying in my desk. I have waited some little time—not long, I admit—but I expected to wait far longer. And, after all, what is having an opera played at Vogelheimsburg? Many have had far greater success than that, and have been forgotten in ten years. Horace has had quite as much success as I. What a conceited ass I must seem to you!"

Theodore took an early opportunity of calling on Vincent, with whom he had always been on terms of mutual civility, though the two men had nothing in common but their interest in Horace Lancaster. Mr. Vincent, who was just returned from a railway committee meeting, did not at all share the anxiety of Horace's wife and sister. "His is an arduous life," he said; "and he is a man who does everything at an unnecessary expense of nervous energy. I am always urging him to husband it a little more. He will learn patience under criticism—he is but little accustomed to unfriendly criticism, you know. The Dockhampton papers were so civil, he has been spoiled. And he is too anxious to succeed; you must give him a little of your philosophy. He has an unfortunate idea that genius consists, to a great extent at least, in a morbid sensitiveness."

"And a morbid seclusion," said Theodore. "One cannot waste much time on society, if one would do anything; but a little of the common light and air are good even for genius."

"That is, as you know, my own idea," said Vincent. "I am not a man of genius, and should speak humbly; but I have never been able to see the wisdom of eccentricity. It is, to say the least of it, a waste of time and energy."

"I am glad that he has been persuaded to undertake the management of his affairs——"

"Why, as to that, Mr. Paston," said Vincent, with a smile which would have been irresistible if it had not slightly increased, or appeared to increase, the very trifling obliquity of his fine eyes; "as to that, I have not entirely succeeded. He has condescended to be placed on the committee, and to attend two or three meetings, but that is about the extent. It is a beginning, however; and I should not advise his plunging into the mysteries of the Stock

Exchange without a little preparation. Even genius is glad sometimes to take a little advice from very commonplace persons."

"Ah, if he had but listened to you, he would long ago have made a name for himself," said Theodore. "You are a master of that common sense which he has always neglected. It is next to genius—I sometimes think that it is genius. With it, a man can do very much what he likes."

"Nay, you glorify it too far. I think, however, that common sense can better afford to do without genius, than genius can afford to do without common sense. Our friend certainly possesses genius, and as certainly does not possess common sense. I have done what I could, and what he would permit me—but there is so much which a man must do for himself," said Vincent thoughtfully. "In the last resort, no one can either help or advise—that, at least, is my experience. Horace has taken more advice from me than most men have from another; but I assure you, I find him immovable on many important points—and I am afraid, increasingly so. However, I shall always believe in his genius, and in his ultimate success. But I agree with you in wishing to defer *Camillus*."

"I shall come to you for advice some of these days, myself," said Theodore, as he took his leave. "Which of the railways do you think is the safest to invest in? One really can't do anything else with one's money now. But moderate interest and certainty are what I want—these tempting prospectuses promise too much."

"I understand," said Vincent laughing. "You want ease of mind, and you are right. I hope that Horace will always be of your opinion—but that's confidential."

CHAPTER X.

Oh what a precious comfort 'tis, to have so many, like brothers, commanding one another's fortunes!—
Timon of Athens.

SINCE Adelaide's illness, a considerable change had come over Mrs. Simpson. She had succeeded in making her peace with Horace, to whom she was extremely attentive while Adelaide was at Twickenham, and had persuaded him that her " unlucky indiscretion," as she called it with the utmost frankness, would have been perfectly harmless but for that unfortunate circumstance at the *Portico,* owing to which poor dear darling Addy had got it into her head that Horace still retained his *penchong* for Lady Fidelle. Horace was not quite clear whether Sophia knew of that unfortunate circumstance or not. Sophia's emotional style of conversation frequently left but a vague impression of facts, but he was satisfied that she had been somehow or other betrayed into her indiscretion out of zeal for himself.

"I did a terribly foolish thing in letting Addy know what you confided to me then about your own feelings," said Sophia, with tears in her eyes. "I'm sure I shall never forgive myself! But who would have thought that the poor dear girl would have taken it so? There was really no harm at all in what I *said*, you know—it was the interpretation she put upon it. As it says so beautifully in *Othello*, 'There's nothing in the world, but thinking makes it so.' In *Hamlet*, is it? Oh yes, of course; I recollect now. Ah! my dear Horace, when shall we see you in *Hamlet* again? *Richard III.* is all very well; but he's such a monster. Your good looks are quite thrown away. I declare I won't go to see you! And every one says you are by far the handsomest *Hamlet* on the stage."

"Man at his best estate is altogether vanity," says the Psalmist; and if the word has slightly changed in meaning, the modern acceptation is no less true than the ancient. Sophia combined flattery with *souchong* of an admirable flavour, poured from the identical teapot which had in former days dispensed hospitality to the doctor.

"I have many associations with that teapot," said Sophia, observing Horace's eyes fixed upon it. "Adelaide's poor dear father bought it for me. This is a world of vicissitudes!" Sophia sighed, but, recovering herself, said in a more sprightly tone, "I am going to ask your advice on a matter that will astonish you."

"I am a very poor adviser."

"My dear Horace," said Sophia decisively, "I know that your modesty leads you to think far too humbly of your own judgment. I am going to confide in you—even the doctor is not to know. He would not oppose me—don't think I would do anything against his wishes

—but he would be anxious. He has the most delightfully old-fashioned notions about the Bank of England, you know, and that sort of thing. He has oceans of money, and can afford to lock it up and get next to nothing for it; but I told him when we married, that I was too poor for the Bank of England. Lambton and Wrench have invested my money for me in something or other—you know, my dear Horace, I never took Mr. Vincent's view about them. Of course, it's all settled on me, and I can do exactly as I like with it. The doctor is most liberal, I must say "—Sophia glanced complacently round the room, and at her own very handsome lilac silk—"but I don't like to be always troubling him; you can understand that, I'm sure. And when everybody's making such a mint of money, it really does seem a sin to leave one's pittance— such as it is—where it gets five per cent. or so. Now it has occurred to me that you can advise me."

"My dear Sophia, you should go to Vincent."

"No, Horace, I prefer coming to you. I have far more confidence in your opinion, and if you don't help me, I shall think you grudge the trouble. Let me give you another cup of tea. Well, now, what do you say?"

"I have really so very little knowledge or experience, Sophia."

"I am quite willing to wait a few weeks, until you have got more," said Sophia gaily. "I know you have begun to turn your attention that way, and I shall expect you to give me the first benefit. I have thought, from the time this railway matter first began to be talked of, that you were eminently fitted to take a prominent part. You must inherit some of dear uncle's business talents."

"I never felt the slightest inclination even to discover whether I had or no, Sophia."

"Well, you have plenty of talent from somewhere," said Sophia laughing. "And why you let Mr. Vincent get such a name for doing what you could so easily have done yourself, passes my comprehension. I suppose you could hardly keep on the theatre if you were in Parliament; but there are many railway directors who are not in Parliament. Well, I look to you to find me some nice shares, that will begin to pay at once!"

It has been remarked that Mrs. Simpson was somewhat changed, and the change was not confined to her ideas upon money matters. Sophia's moral nature was not extraordinarily sensitive, although she very sincerely said of herself that she would on no account do anything which she thought wrong; and, in particular, she was by no means prone to reverence. But she had an unfeigned desire for her husband's good opinion, and she had acutely felt his rebuke. The good doctor had been as kind and considerate as ever—indeed, he had treated her with the tender compassion of a wise parent towards a thoughtless child; but Sophia was well aware that she had fallen in his esteem. Heretofore, he had beheld her as she represented herself to him. The simplicity of his own character and motives gave him no clew to a nature like hers. Even now he would have been startled to hear her called a worldly minded woman. But he was deeply shocked at a mother so far forgetting her instincts as to utter words which she must have known were calculated to destroy her daughter's happiness; and Sophia knew that, simple as the doctor might be in the affairs of this world, it was impossible to persuade him that she was free from moral blame, and guilty only of inadvertence. Sophia had experienced an entirely new sensation. It had never before occurred to her to desire the moral approbation of a fellow-creature. She had desired to be socially correct and respectable, but this is quite another thing. For the first time in her life it was a real pain to her that a most gentle and merciful judge did not wholly approve of her actions.

As Sophia had said, the doctor was extremely liberal, and, but for this new-born sensitiveness, she might never have made up her mind to follow the universal example, and dabble in shares. And Sophia dearly loved a rubber, and, better still, a round game. And the fashions changed so often nowadays, one positively needed three times as many gowns and bonnets in a year as people used ever to dream of having.

The doctor was extremely liberal, to be sure; but Caleb kept his accounts for him, and Caleb was not accustomed to a lady's expenses—poor Sarah never went out. And one never has too much money—let people say what they will about having so much one doesn't know what to do with it. And such splendid opportunities as offered every day! Of course, one would not be rash; but these schemes could not all be unsafe. Sophia had once or twice put into a lottery, and only caution had prevented her doing so oftener. But now she could afford a little risk, and the more she thought about it, the more tempting it seemed to double one's income in a day by a stroke of one's pen.

Horace, after a conference with Vincent as

to the prospects of the Cloppingford Railway Company, recommended it to Sophia, as offering more immediate advantages than the older companies, and greater safety than most of the new ones. He was himself a director, and knew something of the proceedings. His expenses during the last few years had been very great, and in his most sanguine moments he never expected to reimburse himself by the receipts of his theatre. Vincent had always been urging him to take a more active part in the business of the company, and whenever Horace attended a board meeting, would take care to ask his opinion, and draw him into as much prominence as possible. Thanks to the large sums which Horace had at different times invested in the company's shares, and aided by his father's name, and probably also by Vincent's tactics, Horace made a very respectable figure at the board; and if Vincent did most of the work, he knew how to keep that fact somewhat in the background. Sir Saville had retired from the board shortly after the little unpleasantness at the *Portico*, and Vincent had it pretty much his own way with Mr. Copeland, Sir John Overton, and the half-dozen respectable nonentities whose names made a show on the prospectus.

When Adelaide at last insisted on returning to Russell Square, she found Horace's attention more divided than she had ever known it. He would even leave the library (where he might be heard declaiming *Camillus*) to see "a gentleman from the office." Mrs. Staples, whom Caleb often favoured with an evening call, commented on the new turn of affairs, and remarked that it was time he did something, to be sure, to make some money, for he had spent enough, by all accounts, on that theatre, and 'twas but a little place after all.

"You should ha' seen the one at Dockhampton, ma'am," said Caleb. "Three times as big as this one, it was, an' a splendid painting, as big as a pennyrammer, almost, with King Harry the Eighth—him as 'ad so many wives, you know—a-disembarking to go to the Battle of Ajincourt."

"Law, Mr. Caleb, you are a scholar, to be sure!" exclaimed Mrs. Staples, much impressed with the extent of her visitor's information. "Why, you know as much as the doctor, pretty nigh."

"I have picked up a little information on common subjects, Mrs. Staples," said Caleb modestly; "but you must go to the doctor for foreign languages. My old master, Mr. Bolland, was pretty well at home in 'em, but, bless you, the doctor beats him holler. I can remember the doctor, ma'am, when he wore hobnail shoes, and used to come to say his Latten grammar to Mr. Bolland. A very quiet boy he was. I remember, as if it was yesterday, what Mr. Bolland said to me, the first day he ever come with his book. I was a-laying the table for lunch, and Mr. Bolland was a-standing at the window, watching him go down the drive. I can see him now, trudging along, with his shoulders most up to ears, as if he was a-thinking of nothing. 'Caleb,' says Mr. Bolland to me. 'See that boy, Caleb?' says he. 'Yes, sir,' says I. 'The schoolmaster's lad, ain't it, sir?' 'Yes,' says Mr. Bolland. 'And I'm very much mistaken, Caleb, if that boy don't grow to be the village sinecure one day,' says he."

"Law, Mr. Caleb, did he really? Well, it shews what learning can do. But you say the doctor won't have nothing to do with the railways?"

"Mr. Bolland was bit that way, Mrs. Staples—it was before I knew him," said Caleb, disclaiming responsibility. "He dropped a lot o' money, and a burnt child dreads the fire, as they say. For my part, I think circumstances alters cases, Mrs. Staples. Look 'ee here, ma'am!" Caleb drew forth a fat green pocket-book tied round with string, and unfastening it with great deliberation, produced some pieces of paper, of divers colours, and covered with stamps and flourishes. "These are the present issue, and these are the forthcoming issue—they're in the Cloppingford Railway, as you'll see, Mrs. Staples. I thought that was bound to be safe, Mr. Lancaster and Mr. Vincent being on it."

"And I only wish I'd done the same, Mr. Caleb. But, there! I was persuaded by a friend o' mine, last midsummer year, it was, and I put mine in Great Westerns, and now every one tells me it's the wust paying railway there is!"

"Why don't you sell out, ma'am?"

"Why, Mr. Caleb, I don't understand enough about these sort o' things to go meddling here and there. But they was all at me, always saying how silly I was to keep my savings laying idle, so I bought some Great Westerns; but I wish I hadn't!"

CHAPTER XI.

> Let a good actor, in a lofty scene,
> Shew great Alcides honour'd in the sweat
> Of his twelve labours; or a bold Camillus,
> Forbidding Rome to be redeem'd with gold
> From the insulting Gauls; or Scipio,
> After his victories, imposing tribute
> On conquer'd Carthage: if done to the life,
> As if they saw their dangers, and their glories,
> And did partake with them in their rewards,
> All that have any spark of Roman in them,
> The slothful arts laid by, contend to be
> Like those they see presented.
> *The Roman Actor.*

CAMILLUS was Horace's first appearance in a play of his own—for the *Dream* was no more than a recitation in character. There were some effective scenes in the play, and some fine situations; and it would most likely have succeeded, if Horace's reputation had been such as to draw an audience of a different order. It would even have been better if he had made his first appearance in London in *Camillus;* a certain amount of curiosity had been then aroused, which had since subsided. And those adverse criticisms had done him much harm, for the time—and Horace was not of those who know how to wait. If he could have waited, if he could have gone on, patiently doing his best, he might have won a reputation which would have drawn to see *Camillus* an audience capable of appreciating such a play. Horace was not wholly wrong in his bitter complaints of the frequenters of the *Portico.* The theatre was not in a fashionable quarter, and its walls had never echoed to a line of Shakespeare until Horace took it. His task was difficult and laborious, but it need not have been impossible. And he could not plead in excuse of his impatience that he could not afford to wait.

In many respects, *Camillus* deserved to succeed; and Horace's acting had never been so natural. In depicting complex passion, he was apt to be overstrained; but in *Camillus*, that very self-consciousness, which he could so seldom entirely throw off, helped to give the impression of greater dignity and self-restraint. But the play did not take. There was some applause once or twice, particularly at the end of the second act, in which *Camillus*, going into exile, prays that if he be unjustly banished his country may yet need him, and repent her injustice. But the night alarm in the Capitol was not understood—the audience only laughed at the cackling of the geese, and continually interrupted the play by cackling ever after in imitation. Moreover, geese having been introduced, it was too tempting not to hiss a little in the intervals of cackling, though the house was very good-humoured, and even Kiddle did not think it deliberately intended to damn the play. A malicious criticism appeared, in which the critic accused Mr. Lancaster of intolerable conceit for presuming to write *Camillus*, when Shakespeare had written *Coriolanus*.

Horace was furious. On the night of the performance, he was with the utmost difficulty withheld from going before the curtain and telling his audience what he thought of them; and, in spite of the remonstrances of Adelaide, Mr. Kiddle, and Theodore, he wrote an angry letter to the *Express*, which provoked the *Express* into a sarcastic leader on the excessive thinness of the poetical skin, at which Charlotte fairly cried with rage. Charlotte had been so incensed at the criticism, that she had not joined her voice to Adelaide's. Dignified silence was all very well, but who is to know that it *is* dignified? People read the criticism, and think you have nothing to say for yourself! This was Charlotte's view of the question, and for once Vincent took the same.

"I don't see why you should not write the letter," he said. "If you were dependent for your bread on public favour, I should advise you not to make an enemy; but situated as you are, you can well afford to take your own course. And a letter is sometimes an advertisement."

Dr. Simpson had been deeply interested in *Camillus*, and never thoroughly understood why it failed. That that sacred fowl, the goose, could be an object of mere ridicule, and that the audience was unable to grasp the solemnity of the occasion, were ideas which did not appeal to his experience. Long before he had learned the Latin for goose—indeed, probably before he had clearly apprehended wherein geese differed from ducks, the goose had been to him a venerable and ancient bird, whose timely cackle had saved Rome, and whose golden effigy was carried in perpetual gratitude along the Sacred Way. And this heroic incident (the doctor rejected Niebuhr, as at least as apocryphal as the historian he decried) had moved an English audience to nothing but inextinguishable laughter! Truly, it was surprising!

Horace would not play for several nights

after this unfortunate affair. He allowed Kiddle to put something on, but he took no interest in it, and shut himself up in the library to write his letter to the *Express*, refusing even to listen to Kiddle's proposal to leave out the actual cackling, and try *Camillus* once more.

The failure of *Camillus* seemed to have completely unhinged Horace. In vain Theodore urged upon him that a failure was seldom disastrous in itself; that a future success would obliterate it, or possibly even reverse it, and besought him to remember that one may gain invaluable experience through failure. Horace rebelled at the idea of genius needing experience, especially when that experience was to come in the shape of the verdict of his inferiors.

"Would you have me remodel my own conceptions to suit those of the linen-drapers' apprentices in the pit?" he asked indignantly. "They don't care for Shakespeare himself. This is a degenerate age. He was appreciated in his time."

"I don't know much about Shakespeare's life," said Theodore, "but I dare say he had to wait, like the rest of us."

"To wait! yes, but not to be damned. Do you think a line of his was ever hissed?"

"I don't know. But I do know that many of the other great dramatists failed sometimes. Beaumont and Fletcher did not always hit it, nor Ben Jonson himself."

"Their plays are unequal," said Horace; "but they mostly gained attention."

"My dear fellow, pardon my venturing to suggest that you too may be occasionally unequal. Homer nods."

"Yes, but that the pit and the gallery should decide—and that a man who professes to be a man of genius should bid me take their verdict humbly and *profit* by it—profit by the incapacity of fools!"

"I don't profess to be a genius. I can't help writing music, that's all," said Theodore laughing. "And why not profit by fools? Why not learn of them how to make them understand you?"

"I cannot give them an understanding," said Horace loftily. "Would you abase your music to the popular level? If your opera had failed, would you have thought the public knew best?"

"Well, not exactly," said Theodore, with a humorous twitch of his mouth. "But I do say, in all seriousness, that I should have tried as hard to make my second opera better than my first—as I mean to do now!"

"In fact, you are absolutely insensible to criticism, and yet you advise me to take a lesson from it," said Horace in a huff. He very much doubted at the moment whether Theodore had one spark of genius; the sentiments he held pointed rather to his being a man of talent and application only. "I see that genius is a misfortune," he said aloud. "Respectable talent is far more successful than genius, which only serves to raise a man out of reach of the appreciation it is his doom to desire."

"Genius must be patient," said Theodore.

"Genius can never be patient!" cried Horace very impatiently. "Genius sees in a flash what other men toil after and grope after. Genius must be free."

"Who is so free as he who can wait?" said Theodore with kindling eyes. "He sails straight on whither he is bound, not diverted from his course by the winds either of praise or blame. He knows that Time himself is his friend! Dear friend, do not despair so soon. Many have waited and toiled in poverty and obscurity for half a life. You are already known. You have achieved some measure of success. What is this partial failure?"

"No failure can be partial to me," said Horace. "There is no middle place. But you may be partly right. It is possible that I have been too impatient. Theodore, I have wronged you. I thought you calm, indifferent. I see that you at least are not patient, because you have never aspired." Horace was pacing up and down, as he always did when much moved. "Do not think I seek only fame," he said. "'Yet if it be a sin to covet honour'— but the honour I chiefly covet is not that which crowns even a poet. I want to restore the drama—to raise the public taste, and make England what she once was, the very home of dramatic art. Is it impossible that there should ever be another Elizabethan age? Vincent smiles with superior scorn when I speak thus to him. He thinks Stephenson and Hudson are our Shakespeare and Marlowe. I often doubt, dearly as I love him, whether his heart ever throbbed with delight in anything but what he calls the useful. And yet, 'tis strange, his advice agrees with yours. Perhaps I should have listened to him before if he had been less ruthlessly prosaic. He affects it— I am sure of it. He thinks he must be all for reason, since I am all for intuition and passion. But he has erred; a little passion on his part would have moved me more than all his reasonings, which only confirm me in my own view. He knows men well, too."

"Vincent sees all by the sheer force of his

intellect," said Theodore. "He is a terrible man—a man of iron and steel. He is not what we mean by a genius, but he is more infallible than genius itself. He understands even the things he has no sympathy with."

"I will be patient," repeated Horace. "We will put on *Othello*, and I will try to forget that not a score of the audience can grasp my idea, or would care for it if they could. How Shakespeare's soul must have chafed at the groundlings! *He* was not above indulging in a thrust at them. But I will be patient, and, indeed, I have often been rebuked when I thought of you."

"You are too good to say so," cried Theodore much moved—more at something in Horace's manner than by his words.

CHAPTER XII.

Iago. Virtue? a fig! 'tis in ourselves, that we are thus, or thus.

In spite of this mishap, Charlotte's wedding was as merry as could be wished. Horace shook off his gloom, and seemed determined that every one else should forget it too. There had been very serious debates about Theodore's future course, Horace feeling that the *Portico* was too narrow a sphere for his friend's abilities. Theodore however said that it gave him all he wanted—just work enough to prevent his feeling idle.

"I mean composition to be the work of my life," he said, as they were discussing the matter one night not long before the wedding.

"But I cannot compose either so fast or so well when I am entirely my own master. If you turn me adrift, I shall lie on Charlotte's lawn at Twickenham all day, watching the clouds and the boats, thinking sonatas by the dozen, but never writing one. No; let me stay with you, as long as I am in England. Besides, I love you, and could never be happy to sever my fortunes from yours. I shall do more work. I know myself. I am a lazy fellow at bottom, as all artists are, and I need a spur. I wrote an *andante* yesterday, after rehearsal; if I had had the whole day, I should have done no more. I scribbled it down—will you hear it? It is for piano and violin. You had better take the violin, Horace; you can't read my piano score."

"I don't think we could be happier than we are, Addy," whispered Charlotte, as they began the *andante*. Like all Theodore's music, it was full of variety; he availed himself but sparingly of the licence of musicians to repeat themselves. In this *andante*, one passage, full of the most satisfying harmonies, came in again and again with admirable effect. "We seem to rest when that comes," said Charlotte. "It is like lying on one's oars and floating, after rowing hard. Oh, Addy, don't you wish we could hear *Undine?*"

Sophia found Charlotte respond more kindly than Adelaide had done to the calls of fashion, but she had the wedding dress made "ridiculously plain," and she travelled in a Leghorn instead of a Pamela bonnet, on the plea that it suited her better. Sophia would also have preferred that the wedding should take place in town, instead of at Twickenham, and thought it a very insufficient reason that dear uncle Lancaster had spent his own honeymoon at Riverside House. But the day was fair— one of the very few fine days of that winter of fog and rain; the wedding was pretty, and the doctor assisted in the ceremony. The Vincents were not there—they were at Overton; but Captain Overton came down to be his cousin's best man, and Hannah and Sally Hillyard were Charlotte's bridesmaids. Mr. and Mrs. McLasher (*née* Sophy Hillyard) were also of the party. Mr. McLasher had good stories to tell of everybody, including Lady Overton and Sir Saville Fidelle (these latter when the captain was not by). Sophia perceived, with regret, that he too was infatuated with Vincent's cleverness. Mr. Hillyard himself was unable to come; he had been laid up with an attack of gout, and was afraid to venture on the journey, but he sent Charlotte a handsome pair of silver candlesticks as a wedding present.

The new-married couple intended to spend their honeymoon and Christmas at Vogelheimsburg, as Theodore naturally wished to introduce his bride to his parents, and it was several years since he had spent a Christmas with them.

Horace and Adelaide returned to town immediately after the wedding. He had some thought of attempting *King Lear,* but he felt that for this a long and careful preparation would be necessary, and he resolved to play in several less tragic parts before he made so ambitious a venture. Theodore had strongly advised him to produce *Measure for Measure,* instead of another tragedy, and Horace had only hesitated because he feared Miss Elton was not quite equal to the part of *Isabella.* In the meanwhile he was playing *Hamlet* to tolerable houses.

The Cloppingford railway was in course of construction, and was to be opened in the autumn. The rains did some damage to a tunnel, and caused a little delay, but Vincent on his return to town made very little of this, and confirmed the report that Hudson would consent to be chairman of the board. Mr. Vincent, however, was to be deputy-chairman; and, as it was impossible that Hudson could devote much personal attention to the general business, the brunt of the work would fall on Vincent.

Horace's tragedies had been noticed favourably in several quarters, and Adelaide triumphantly reminded him of how Theodore had always said he had only to wait until he was better known. Some of the reviewers appeared hardly to be aware that Horace was anything but what he described himself on the title page—"barrister-at-law." After all, said Adelaide, the time was very short—most of the actors whose names every one knew had been upon the stage years and years. "You will be a great man by the time Horry is able to read Shakespeare," she said, smiling up at her husband, as she sat with their little girl upon her knee.

"What an *Isabella you* would make, Adelaide!" cried Horace. "You need nothing but a little confidence. I sometimes think it would have been better for me if I had been in want of money as well as of fame. Then, too, you would have helped me. We may come to it yet," he added, half laughing. "I have dissipated my substance more than I like to think of, and if it were not for the Cloppingford Railway, we should be obliged to cut down our expenses somewhere."

There was one exception to the kindly tone of the reviewers. The *Express* tore the tragedies limb from limb, called them specimens of inflated bombast, and was glad to know that the public taste had not yet sunk so low as to mistake verbiage for poetry and bathos for pathos—it was glad to be able to inform lovers of genuine tragedy that one at least of these plays (and not the worst) had been speedily hissed off the stage of a third-rate little theatre, not a hundred miles from the Edmonton Road.

Horace forgot even his dignity in his indignation at this abominable and unjustifiable attack, as he called it. It proceeded from personal enmity. He had a great mind to bring an action for libel. "Look there!" he said, thrusting the *Express* into Vincent's hands (he had hurried to Bloomsbury Square as soon as he had read the obnoxious critique).

"See what the fellow dares to say! It is infamous that a gentleman who is devoting his life to the best interests of the drama should be insulted in this manner by a penny-a-liner! Read it for yourself!"

Vincent read: "'Mr. Lancaster has been before the public for some little time as a bad actor; he now comes before it as a bad playwright. In both capacities he displays the same over-weening self-confidence, in both he prefers sound to sense; as an actor, he mouths; as a poet—save the mark!—he rants. We dismiss him—to the *Portico!*'"

"Well!" exclaimed Horace impatiently, when he saw that Vincent's eyes had travelled to the end of the paragraph. "What do you say to it?"

"These things are said pretty much at haphazard of anybody, I fancy," said Vincent. "The writer chooses to say you are bombastical—perhaps he does not think so, or perhaps he does. No one can prove that he does, or does not. It is simply a question of whether most of those who read your poetry agree with him."

"Dick, I would not have believed you could be so cold in a matter which concerns me so nearly!"

"My dear Horace, I am no judge of poetry, and never professed to be. You always write good grammar, and each of your sentences conveys a certain meaning. Each of your plays contains more or less of a story which is perfectly comprehensible. For instance, you shew us Camillus, a successful general, banished by the enemies he had made by his arrogant manners, and afterwards returning with an army to deliver Rome from an invasion of the Gauls, and restored to all his honours. This is the story which you tell in your play. You represent Camillus himself as a man of great energy and talent, who rendered himself obnoxious to the plebeians. He does not attempt to maintain his position by stirring up disorder in the state, always a dangerous game, and which, as Rome then was—whatever weight we may allow to Livy—could not possibly have succeeded. He evidently felt pretty sure that he would be wanted again, and the event proved him right. You shew this and much more quite plainly enough— of this I can judge. But as to those less tangible literary beauties which we call poetry, I cannot pretend to decide. I admire a well-written book, but I confess that prose gives me more pleasure than poetry, and I have always said so frankly, as I have a great dislike to be found out."

"Dick," said Horace solemnly, "even this cruel attack gives me less pain than so unworthy a view of a great man's character as you have just taken. I am a bad playwright, indeed, if I have represented Camillus as the calculating politician you describe! I cannot tell you, Dick, how your persistent ignoring of all but selfish motives in mankind chills and grieves me. Do you not believe there is such a thing as magnanimity?"

"My dear Horace, it is easy to use high-flown language. I believe that we all seek pleasure and avoid pain. Many of us do so far less consciously than others; the dull-brained snatch at the good most easy of attainment, with little regard to consequences, while more far-seeing persons look ahead and see that the good of the moment will soon result in positive evil. But the motives of both wise men and fools are the same. My dear Horace, life is a game of chess, in which most people see only one, or at most two moves ahead; a few see almost the whole game; and a very few indeed know how to force every move of their adversary."

"Yet, Dick, I think when you pulled me out of the Isis, you had not much time to calculate the consequences of saving me. Then, at least, you acted on a mere generous, unreasoning impulse, such as you now deny the existence of."

"We are members of society, not savages," said Vincent. "Long experience has taught us that the prosperity of others is often a distinct advantage to ourselves. So firmly is this principle established, that we punish as a criminal the man who tries to serve himself except by contributing in some way to the general good. Society blames the manner, but not the motive; the banker as well as the thief serves himself, but the thief offers no equivalent to society in return. I grant the existence of instincts—I fully admit that a civilized man's first thought on seeing any one in need is usually to assist him."

"But you consider his instinct to be only a development of the original instinct of self-preservation?"

"Self-preservation is the first law of nature," said Vincent, smiling at Horace's vehemence. "Do not be angry, Horace. You know me well enough to know that so enlightened a doctrine of self-interest as I hold, comes to very much the same thing as your own more high-flown creed."

"I shall never love your doctrine, Dick," said Horace; "luckily, your deeds are more disinterested than your words."

CHAPTER XIII.

Oh these railroad speculations! and this mania after gain!
I think the time is fully come when wives may now complain.
Talk of German wool and polkas, mesmeric tastes and singing;
What are they to the fearful ills from speculation springing?
My husband, once he was so gay, but he's so altered now—
He looks as if he bore the weight of nations on his brow.

  * * * * * *

His head seems quite bewildered; 'twas but the other day,
Instead of boys, he bid me send "the Glosters out to play."
And when I asked, for dinner would he like beef-soup or fish?
He said, "My love, some Exeters, or any shares you wish."

To watch him with the newspapers, a terror 'tis to me—
He reads, and mutters, " Sheffield's up, and Midland's
  down, I see ;
Great Westerns, what a rise they've made! Oh, had I
  kept that lot,
On an advance like this, I should two thousand pounds
  have got!"
The Wife's Complaint.

EVER since the extraordinary excitement in the share-market early in February, there had been an occasional tendency to panic, but hitherto the only result had been to fan the flame of speculation. But many signs may be detected of a growing doubt, hardly as yet to be called suspicion, of foul play somewhere or other—no one knows where. We may read for instance in the newspapers of the day, that "some slight suspicion is abroad" that the knowledge of the lines recommended by the Board of Trade finds its way into the market before the announcements appear in the *Gazette.*" And "stags" begin to be talked about. A "stag" is explained to be a person who contrives to raise shares to a premium, and then to pocket that premium. By this means it is said that some one (of course everybody has a shrewd guess as to who it is) has cleared £100,000 in a day. This illustrious monarch of the glen sees no harm in it; and perhaps many persons who may read this history would be puzzled to express the harm of trying to make bricks without straw—until they hear of the crash which was, and is, and always will be, the final result of staggery in whatever disguise. Brougham too had some time since reminded the Lords again of 1825. But there are great public questions in plenty to divert Brougham and everybody else from inquiring too nicely into staggery. There is Mr. Disraeli firing off an epigram a night at Sir Robert, and sarcastically reminding him that three courses are open to us—"the course the right hon. gentleman is following, the course the right hon. gentleman has left, and the course the right hon. gentleman ought to pursue." And while the corn-law battle rages fiercer and fiercer, and the bray of Exeter Hall rises against the endowment of Maynooth, Sir John

Franklin sails away to the North Pole, like Humphrey Gilbert, to return no more. But—

> "Heaven is as near
> By water as by land."

Mr. O'Connell, too, with his Head Pacificator (who pacifies in rather strong language), is entering Cork in triumph, to the music of the identical harp that once on Tara's hill the soul of union shed, played before him by a venerable person sitting under an oak in a waggon. And a little later, everybody is talking about the railway gauge question, and Mr. Hudson's election at Sunderland, of which the news is brought by the *Times* express in eight hours.

So desperate is the eagerness in Leeds, that the police have to keep the approaches to the three Stock Exchanges, which are like so many fairs. And all over the country, draughtsmen, lithographers, printers, and engravers are working at the plans of the new lines, which must be sent in by the 30th of November. The older railways are forced, in self-defence, to join in schemes they were too cautious to originate, and to open new branches, which they never expect will pay, in order to prevent rival lines being started, which would ruin their traffic. So freely did money pour in at this time, that companies were able to pay high interest even before their lines were made. In watching the ascent of the bubbles, people almost forgot to replenish the bowl. The making of the lines was less talked of by the great body of scrip and share holders, than were the quotations of shares in the market, the probable amount of the premiums, and the effect which the starting of some new company would be likely to produce upon prices.

The excitement had long since spread through all ranks of society. There are caricatures of Alfred Crowquill's, showing omnibuses crowded inside and out with passengers, every man of them buried in an enormous newspaper. At last, the caricaturist represents a newspaper so large that it covers a good-sized garden, and ladies and gentlemen walk up and down the columns, and follow the lines of print with stick and parasol, to see whether Exeters have fallen, or Newcastle-and-Darlingtons have risen. People sat up all night, waiting in coffee-houses for the publication of the *Gazette*, to see which line Government would consider first. Wild-eyed listeners gathered round to hear the *Gazette* read; ruin or fortune hung upon the order of the names. Those mysterious rumours, anticipating the *Gazette*, became more frequent; now and then they happened to be true, so false ones multiplied, and a still more disastrous phase of the universal madness was entered on. The kingdom was a great stock exchange. In one month four hundred and fifty-seven new plans were registered, each plan a fresh centre of stock-jobbing, staggery, and all the wheels within wheels, and wheels within wheels again, which lie snugly concealed in the innocent-seeming word, " speculation." A series of accidents—several fatal—

brought up Colonel Sibthorpe to move for a return of killed and wounded, and to compare railways to civil wars. The scramble for wealth was too fierce for the scramblers to pay much heed to Colonel Sibthorpe; but louder voices than his were about to speak. Just when the frenzy of gambling was at its height, and when the whole commercial fabric, like a house of cards, tottered and shook with its own weight, the Bank of England suddenly raised the rate of discount from $2\frac{1}{2}$ to 3 per cent.; and the *Times* began to fulminate those terrible leading articles, which one who knew what he was saying, compared to "hand-grenades thrown into a camp during a feast."

CHAPTER XIV.

Honour! What's that? 'Tis but a specious title
We should not prize too high.
The Lovers' Progress.

MRS. STAPLES had been considerably disturbed by the comet, and thought that it most likely had something to do with the accidents on the railways. Caleb, however, who had heard that celestial body discussed from an astronomical point of view, doubted whether a score or two of the inhabitants of this planet would count for much, dead or alive, at the other end of the universe, whence he understood the comet to have come; for which opinion the housekeeper pronounced him unfeeling.

Sanguine persons said that only the inevitable reaction from a long period of excitement caused the ugly rumours which had lately been whispered. But early in October, Vincent came one morning while Horace was still at breakfast, looking unusually grave. He said nothing of his errand until Adelaide left the room; but then instantly began—

"You have paid up all your Cloppingford shares, have you not? But I know you have, long since."

"I've got seventy thousand in the Cloppingford Railway—why do you ask?"

"Because I'm not satisfied. A great many of the shareholders have not paid up. It's not my fault; I always said that we ought to allow a much smaller percentage of unpaid shares. But I am very much afraid that a panic is at hand, and if so, the brunt of the loss would fall on you—you are by very much the largest shareholder."

"Dick! Have you reasons for thinking so, or is it merely a surmise?" said Horace looking very uneasy.

"It is partly a surmise; but two or three things I have heard all point in one direction. We have been going very fast, it must be owned; and if people once get thoroughly frightened, there will be a panic. What I advise is, that you sell your shares as quietly as possible. I'll get it done so that your name does not appear. Cloppingfords are higher than ever, thanks to Hudson's election, and you will easily find purchasers. Of course, we shall split up your shares—not attempt to sell them in a lump."

"I suppose you mean to say that I shall lose my money if I don't?" asked Horace.

"I don't go so far as to say that; but I think you have got too much money in the railway. You can leave five thousand or so in, if you prefer it—perhaps it would be better to do so."

"Dick, I want to know clearly whether I am selling because there is danger?"

"Well, yes; I suppose so," said Vincent,

as if he did not see the drift of Horace's question. "You might as well leave it where it is getting as good as 10 per cent., if you were perfectly sure it was safe."

"Suppose there were a panic, what would the shares be worth?"

"Quite impossible to say. The probabilities are that, if there were a panic, every one would be afraid to buy at any price."

"Then, Dick, I must take my chance. I cannot honourably sell shares which I know may be worth nothing in a week."

For once, Vincent looked astounded. "The buyer must see to that. You are not bound to consult his interest; and besides," he added hastily, as he saw that Horace was going to interrupt him, "it may actually pay him to hold them. You forget that I advised you not to sell in a lump. A few thousands——"

"A poor man may buy them, and be ruined. Dick, I won't do it; and I heartily repent having ever meddled with a concern in which such things are thought fair."

Vincent tried in vain to shake his resolve, and was obliged to be content with exacting a promise from Horace to be silent on the subject of the Cloppingford Railway. This promise weighed much on Horace's mind with regard to Sophia, who had invested all her money in shares; but he felt that Vincent had a right to demand secrecy, as the best chance of avoiding the panic he feared. And he reflected that he would, if the worst happened, be able to make up Sophia's loss. She had invested her money at his advice; and his pride no less than his honour forbade the idea that she should lose by so doing.

Horace had been playing in comedy for some months, but was now about to return to more congenial tragedy, and was to re-open the *Portico* with *Othello*. Great pains had been taken with the rehearsals, and Horace was in better spirits than he had been in since *Camillus* failed. *Othello* was his favourite part; and Theodore had the promise of a friendly notice in a newspaper of quite as much importance as the *Express*, which had let Horace alone of late. Vincent would not be in town for the first night; he had gone down to Bleasbrook to see Mr. Copeland, and to make some arrangements for the opening of the railway. Vincent's exertions had been untiring; he had been constantly going to and fro between Cloppingford and London for many months past; and Horace had only seen him at board meetings, and at hasty interviews at home in the intervals of his journeys. Vincent had seemed rather less apprehensive the last time Horace exchanged a word with him on the subject; but he was evidently anxious, and Horace found his thoughts wandering from *Othello* to the share markets, and the probable traffic on the new line, now rapidly approaching completion— sometimes too to vain regrets that he had gone to work so lavishly at Dockhampton, in the confidence of speedy success. Horace had a few days since brought home his deed-box from Vincent's, in whose custody it had been all the time he was at Dockhampton. He found his attention so distracted by the sight of it (his father's name was still painted on it), that he pushed it out of sight into the shadow of the window-curtain. It was a very new experience to find business cares obtruding themselves thus. Horace threw *Othello* aside at last, and in desperation devoted a precious morning to the task of looking over the documents, preparatory to a consultation with Vincent on some matters of business not connected with the railway.

Amelia called in Russell Square the day that Vincent left town. She had a letter from Lina, in Paris, with a great deal of news of her own and Gerald's doings, which Amelia was to be sure and tell Adelaide. There was also some account of a brief visit from Blanche, with an uncomplimentary allusion to Sir Saville, which Amelia blundered into the middle of before she was aware.

" The part I was to read to you is farther

on," said she, rather confused. "Gerald says he always was the most disagree—— I can't find what she says about you—oh, here it is! 'We shall be in a great hurry to hear how *Othello* goes off. Theodore said in his last letter it was nearly ready.' I shall be very dull till Richard comes back," said Amelia, when she had finished Lina's letter.

"I hope Mr. Vincent is well?" said Adelaide, who always carefully observed the conventional civilities towards Vincent. We are generally careful to be more polite in proportion as we love less.

"Quite well, thank you, Addy dear. Though really perhaps I ought not to say so. He woke me in the night in such a fright— it was the oddest thing. I never was so terrified in my life."

"Was he ill?"

"No, he was only dreaming; but he never does dream—never. I've often asked him, and he always says he *never* dreams. But last night he woke me moaning, and saying, 'another?' 'another?' in such a hoarse, dreadful voice. I shook him, to wake him, and even when he woke he was all of a tremble. I made him tell me the dream, and the oddest part was that there was really nothing at all dreadful in it—nothing. And yet he was moaning as if he were being killed."

"What was it? May you tell me?" said Adelaide, smiling involuntarily at the incongruous idea of Mr. Vincent troubled by a nightmare.

"Oh yes, there was hardly anything to tell. He only dreamed that he was in some great room like a library, but very large—an enormous room, full of books right up to the ceiling. He was going, he thought, to look for something that was in only one book. He knew the book, because it had red letters on the back that shone like fire. He dreamed that he found the book, and tore out a certain leaf—he didn't know why he did it, but he had to do it in his dream. Well, he had torn out the leaf, and he was coming away, when he saw another book with fiery letters on its back, and he knew that he must tear a leaf out of that too. And when he had done that, there was another—the red letters kept appearing on fresh books in all parts of the library—wherever he looked there was sure to be a book with these red letters. He dreamed that he tore out leaves till he was tired; but it was of no use—the red letters sprang out of the backs of hundreds of books at least— they got to be more and more instead of fewer, as he tore out the leaves. I suppose it was the nightmare, but when *I* have it, I always dream of mad bulls or something frightful. There's nothing very dreadful in books. Richard wouldn't believe me this morning when I told him what he had said—he declared it was all a dream of my own. He had forgotten all about it."

Just then Horace came in. "I must have a rest," he said when he had greeted Amelia. "I feel good for nothing. I have done nothing all the morning, and yet I do not know when

I have felt so exhausted. Give us some music, Adelaide. Amelia has not heard that song of mine which Theodore set to music last week."

CHAPTER XV.

> I do fear,
> When every feather sticks in his own wing,
> Lord Timon will be left a naked gull.
> *Timon of Athens.*

HORACE had received an official intimation of an extraordinary meeting of the board of directors, to be held the day before Vincent left town; but he was so engrossed in his theatrical duties that he forgot all about the meeting for several days, and attached no particular meaning to the words written opposite the printed formula, "*Business of the Meeting,*" "Inquiry as to cheques drawn on Dean and Webster." Dean and Webster were the company's bankers; Horace and his father before him had banked with them also.

Ever since that conversation which Vincent had with him, Horace had anxiously turned every morning to that page of the *Times* on which the magic heading, "MONEY MARKET" appears. The ominous words, "fluctuation in scrip," and hints at "some alarm that money would become suddenly scarce," had caused him a flutter at the heart which he had hitherto seldom felt, except while he awaited his cue at the wings. But now, money was said to be "tolerably easy" again, and even the step taken by the Bank in England in raising the rate of discount, said to have for its object the checking of railway speculation, was lightly spoken of. "A more harmless demonstration could scarcely be devised," said men on the Stock Exchange, the day before their house crumbled about their ears. But Horace had only to turn to another page of the *Times* to read warnings so plain that every widow and spinster who had risked her all in the railway lottery could understand them. Many of the schemes, said the *Times*, in the plainest of plain English, were based on fraud. There were among the directors of the new railways some most notorious scamps and swindlers, who never possessed a penny in the world, and never would possess one by honest means.

"But all your directors are honest men, Horace, are they not?" said Adelaide, when he had read this and much more to the same effect. "You knew them all before?"

"Not all; there are some I know nothing of. But I do not, for an instant, believe the company comes under this condemnation. The *Times* refers to the many bubble companies which are taking advantage of the great activity in the Stock Exchange. Still, these statements must injure all shares; people will inevitably be alarmed. We shall not be absolutely ruined—I have taken care of that," said Horace, smiling at Adelaide's dismayed face. "But we may be much poorer than we have been, if things go wrong. I might even be obliged to sink from a manager to a mere actor. I think I shall take a leaf from Willoughby's book, and seek a provincial engagement, on the strength of my reputation at the *Portico;* it is not entirely worthless— the *Express* could not quite crush me. What do you say, Adelaide, if I become a strolling player; will you go on the boards? Together we should make a sensation, I promise you! I have longed to have you to act with me, ever since I first perceived your resemblance to *Calliope.* I could soon give you all the needful training. I protest, 'twould almost make up for the loss of fortune. With you in *Isabella,* I could work out my conception of *Angelo,* as I have never yet been able to do. They say Garrick declared he often missed half his points by the fault of actresses who would not, or could not, act up to him. All through my career, I have laboured under that disadvantage. Well, I hope much from *Othello.*"

The next was the eventful day, and Horace

gave himself up to his part, and strove by every means to work himself into the fervid mood befitting *Othello*. But he complained that he felt flat and depressed; some little details had gone wrong at the theatre, and the putting them right broke the spell he had been trying to weave round himself, and reduced him, as he said, "to miserable commonplace."

Theodore consoled him by saying that he would feel the enthusiasm come when he needed it. "The music of the overture will be enough to drive away despondency. Music prepares the actors no less than the audience. You will be lifted out of the commonplace soon enough."

"Yes; my passion always grows with the music," said Horace, warming even as he spoke. "But, to-day, I feel as *Hamlet* should, not as *Othello*. I wish it were to be *Hamlet*—I could so intimately express his melancholy sense of doom, and the half-rebellious, half-submissive mood in which he meets it! He is passive in the depths of his soul, and yet he seeks his doom. I never understood him so deeply as to-day, nor sympathized so intensely with the man who could not think and act at the same time; whose thoughts stop short of action, and whose actions, when he is goaded to the point of action, are mere unthinking madness. But 'tis the acutest grief of man's strange, contradictory nature, that performance must ever fall so far short of intention!"

Despite all Horace's laments, his *Othello* that night surpassed all his previous efforts. His grasp of the character was firmer, less spasmodic; he depended less upon minute details, and more upon his conception of the character as a whole, than when he last played it.

At the same time, his fine person and bearing appealed to even those of his audience on whom his other merits might have made less impression.

The next day was Sunday. Horace spent

the afternoon, as usual, in the drawing-room. He had been talking to Adelaide about some poems which he had written in his college days, and had gone downstairs to look for one or two of them which he wished to read to her, when Mrs. Simpson was announced. Adelaide had been thinking, in the few minutes she was alone, that this was perhaps the beginning of success, and hoping that his excitement and irritability would calm down as he began to feel his claims acknowledged and his efforts rewarded. Horace was quiet this afternoon, out of sheer exhaustion after the tremendous strain of last night. He lived in a perpetual unrest, and was generally melancholy when his inspiration left him. Out of this pleasant dream of troubles past, and tranquillity to come, Sophia's very first words awoke her, innocent as they were.

"What a sultry day, to be sure, for the time of year! I feel quite faint. There's another shower! Who would think this was October?" she began; and then, in a lowered voice, the instant the servant had closed the door, "Where's Horace? What does he say about it? What! Haven't you heard that there's a panic in the Stock Exchange, and half the country ruined, they say? Mark my words, Addy, Vincent's at the bottom of it! I don't mean there aren't others as bad, but he's one of them; and if we lose our money, I shall always say so. I warned you from the first—— My dear Horace, what *is* this dreadful news? What *does* it mean? and *is* there anything in it?"

"Pray explain yourself, Sophia," said Horace, smiling at her vehemence. He held several manuscript books in his hand, and was rather sorry to have his afternoon with Adelaide thus broken in upon. "Has Caleb been making love to Mrs. Staples? I see he has just done her the honour of a visit."

"Pray be serious, Horace; it is most *dreadful* news, if true. I heard it from my old friend Major Wiggleston, as we were coming out of church, and he always gets the latest news at his club."

The *Times* had done it all. These leading articles had frightened people out of their wits, it seemed, and everybody was trying to sell his shares, while nobody wanted to buy. There was a regular rush yesterday, and shares down to nothing. "And they'll be lower still to-morrow," continued Sophia. "The major says there's certain to be a panic. They were advertising engineering instruments for sale yesterday! As the major says, that'll shew what we may expect! And it would have been such a nice thing to have one's money in shares, and get premiums every now and then! I'm sure, to read the prospectuses!—— And now these swindlers who have got mixed up with it have spoilt it all! It's enough to provoke a saint! I shall be ashamed to look the doctor in the face when he knows!"

Horace had moved to the window. He did not speak for a minute or two after Sophia had ceased. She sat looking at him, as if impatient for an answer.

"I hope your news will prove to have been

exaggerated," he said at last. "I feel myself in part responsible for having advised you, and, if anything short of ruin befalls me, I shall feel bound to bear you harmless."

Adelaide's face crimsoned and her eyes filled as Horace said this. She felt that for all misfortunes she could only love him more, and be more proud that she loved him.

"I'm sure it's most generous of you to say so, my dear Horace; but of course it's quite out of the question," cried Sophia with a laugh and a little blush. "I'm sure the doctor would never hear of it! I'm sure I don't know how I shall tell him—not that he'll say anything—he is far too much the gentleman for that. There couldn't be a greater contrast than there is between him and the poor major in money matters, I'm sure!"

"Do you think it is so bad as mamma says, Horace?" asked Adelaide after another pause.

"I don't know—Vincent seemed to expect something of the kind a fortnight ago. But in any case, I believe Cloppingford shares will only be depreciated for a time. The railway is to be opened in a week, or less. Ours is a very different thing from these bubble companies. Vincent has always insisted on its being conducted on a solid foundation, and he has always been able to put down any attempts to imitate the doubtful expedients some companies have resorted to. I do not much fear any but a temporary inconvenience."

"You heard what Horace let out about Vincent," said Sophia, as she bade Addy good-bye. "If anything happens, he'll be at the bottom of it—but it's too late to say anything now. It's my belief we are all in a pretty pickle, and thanks to Vincent that we are!"

CHAPTER XVI.

Iago. Knavery's plain face is never seen, till us'd.

MONDAY morning's post brought a letter from Mr. Hillyard, to tell Horace that McLasher had heard a report a few days ago that "all was not square" in the Cloppingford Railway Company. McLasher could learn no details; "but depend upon it, there's something ugly been going on," said Hillyard. There was also a note from Vincent, pleading excess of business as an excuse for not having called, hoping *Othello* had gone off well, and asking Horace to make a point of attending the board meeting next day. Horace had received an official summons to this meeting, on Saturday; the business was stated to be, as before, "to inquire into cheques on Dean and Webster."

The *Times* confirmed Sophia's news only too fully. But worse was to come. Saturday was but the prelude to Monday, when the panic set in like a flood, and, like a flood, swept everything before it. Advertisements, which had flaunted for weeks in all the papers, were suddenly withdrawn—but, to be sure, it had been proposed to punish the *Times* by sending no more advertisements to its columns. But companies disappeared also. In one railway company, thirty directors were *non inventi*. Letters were returned. The *Times* had told the world a few days since, that the 1,428 railway projects represented an outlay of £701,243,208; but many of the companies had been contriving to do with scarcely any outlay at all. One company had sixty pounds in hard cash, and seven hundred thousand on paper! People had been bribed to take shares. Dividends had been paid out of capital. Fictitious shareholders had been invented to swell the directors' majority, and shareholders, scarcely less fictitious for having a physical entity, were accredited with shares to an enormous amount, for which they had not paid a halfpenny in the pound. Men wrote for shares in the names of children, and then sold the letters at fabulous prices; they hung about the share-market, ready to sign for shares to any amount; and these shams were deliberately winked at. One of the worst results of speculation is that it admits of such infinitesimal shades of dishonesty. It is almost impossible to say where one begins to sail a very little near the wind, and quite impossible to draw the line at any one point of the stock-broking compass. Now that the crash had actually begun, and the golden age, when no one stopped to ask questions, was past, there were many devices left whereby something could be saved from the wreck. Some of "the leading City men," as one account euphuistically calls them, cleared twenty-five thousand each, by the simple expedient of returning the deposits and keeping the premiums. Directors made fictitious sales of their own shares to their own brokers, to keep up the appearance of a demand, and thus caught new shareholders even after the panic had begun.

Next to his pocket, every one was anxious to save his reputation, and to assure his neighbours and the public that he had had no idea at all that this sort of thing was going on! Whitecross Street and Queen's Bench were crowded with prisoners. There were four hundred writs out against one gentleman. A peer of the realm betook himself to his yacht; all who could, made themselves scarce. Meanwhile, Mr. Hudson (against whom as yet only the *Yorkshireman* wagged its tongue) was dining in great glory, under his own likeness framed in laurels, in the Polytechnic Hall in Sunderland, and congratulating his new constituents on having defeated the machinations of the Anti-Corn-Law League and Colonel Thompson. And despite the commotion in the Stock Exchange, the young gentlemen with theodolites continued to survey the country, assisted when necessary by dark lanterns and even pistols.

The meeting of directors was larger than usual. Although the company hoped to stand its ground, things looked very black. And to make matters worse, about a fortnight ago a very disagreeable discovery had been made. The contractor for the railway, on presenting a cheque for a large amount on Dean and Webster, had been told that the company had considerably overdrawn its account. This of course led to an explanation, and it had come out at the first extraordinary meeting, that several of the company's cheques had been paid by the bank to some person or persons unknown, which cheques were undoubtedly forgeries. They all bore the names of Mr. Vincent and of two other directors, one of whom was Horace. The bank-manager had stated that he should have mentioned the circumstance of the company's overdrawing, when the last of these forged cheques was presented, had it not borne the name of Mr. Lancaster, who was an old client, and a man of very substantial fortune. It further appeared that while the forger had very clumsily imitated the signatures of Vincent and the other director (who, by-the-bye, was Mr. Copeland), he had succeeded so perfectly with Mr. Lancaster's, as to defy suspicion.

"It was that which deceived us," continued the manager. "We were familiar with Mr. Lancaster's handwriting, and seeing that was all right, we naturally concluded the others were. You'll observe, gentlemen, that Mr. Lancaster's signature is rather remarkable— he writes a bold hand, with a good many flourishes."

As much as thirty thousand pounds had been taken out of the bank at different times, and there seemed no reason to doubt that the guilty party intended to continue his system, and had only been discovered by the accident of the contractor's cheque covering more than the balance left in the bank.

"If I had had the least idea of this, I should have made a point of attending the first meeting," said Horace to the gentleman who had told him all this, and who looked at him rather curiously. "It is a most extraordinary thing. My signature is not an easy one to imitate. It certainly would have deceived me — I can detect no difference." Horace had written his name on a sheet of paper, and was comparing it with the forgery.

One or two of the directors, who were unknown to him, looked at each other, and shrugged their shoulders.

"It is a most unpleasant affair," said one.

"Very much so," said another.

Then Vincent came in, greeted Horace with peculiar warmth, and took his seat in the chair. The solicitor to the Committee of Bankers for Protection against Forgeries, was then introduced, and a great deal was said again which had been said before. The cheques had been drawn for amounts varying from five to ten thousand pounds. They were made payable to different persons—once or twice to the contractor himself. There was nothing remarkable in the withdrawal of these or even larger sums, by a company well known to be constructing a new line. The bank clerks had been questioned, but could not swear to the person or persons who had presented the cheques; but it seemed that some one wearing coloured glasses had presented at least three of them. A tall man, dressed like a gentleman, and wearing blue spectacles, of the kind worn by persons whose eyesight was affected—this was the utmost description elicited by the most minute inquiries, and even here there seemed to be a doubt. The bank had a large connection, and business had been remarkably brisk of late—one man might well have been confused with another.

Horace was exceedingly annoyed, and expressed the most anxious desire that the mystery should be cleared up. Every one agreed that such a thing happening at this critical juncture was a most unfortunate thing, and calculated to greatly injure the company's credit—especially as there was but too much reason to think that the forger must be one who was intimately acquainted with all the company's proceedings. Indeed, it seemed impossible that an outsider could have done it. Mr. Copeland was laid up with the gout, but had sent a long letter of apology for not coming up to town, and declared himself willing to bear one-third of any expenses that might be incurred "in bringing the rascal to justice." Vincent displayed throughout the most admirable coolness. He seemed to forget that one of the names was his—a fact which Horace evidently never lost sight of for an instant in his own case —and his suggestions were more valuable than those of every one else put together. It was at first supposed that cheques drawn for smaller amounts had been altered to larger, but more minute inquiry tended to the conclusion that blank cheques had been fraudulently filled up. It had frequently happened that checks had been filled in, and sent to an absent director for his signature. Although Mr. Lancaster had taken a comparatively inactive part as a director, he had signed a good many cheques —Mr. Vincent having suggested, at an early stage of the company's existence, that it was desirable to have cheques signed by directors known to be substantial men. For this reason, Mr. Copeland, Sir John Overton, Mr. Lancaster, and two or three more, had usually put their names. Cheques were almost always signed by two directors besides the chairman.

These facts, and the singular circumstance that Mr. Lancaster's bold and characteristic signature had been imitated so much more successfully than either Mr. Copeland's rather indistinct, or Mr. Vincent's plain, straightforward hand (both of which forgeries a little examination sufficed to detect), were looked at in every possible light, and commented on with very varying degrees of acuteness by every one present. Mr. Lancaster said more than once that he should have sworn without hesitation to his own signatures. The meeting was about to disperse, when Mr. Pike (the gentleacting on behalf of the Bankers' Protection Committee), stepped up to the chairman, and begged to speak with him in private.

Pike was a sharp-faced man, with a manner which (perhaps intentionally) conveyed the impression that he saw far more deeply into the matter in hand than any of the persons to whom he put his brief, abrupt questions. "Copeland was Member for Cloppingford?" said Pike, when Vincent had led the way into another room. " Lancaster's father was an East India Director "—Pike was jotting down a few words in his note-book while he spoke— " a barrister, I think ? And has taken to the stage, and must have lost a good deal of money on it, I should think "—here Pike licked his pencil, and turned a new leaf. " Several years at Dockhampton. Spent a good deal there?"

"I am afraid so," said Vincent. "Mr. Lancaster has an idea of reforming the stage altogether, and I'm afraid he has gone too fast for the public to follow him."

"Just so," said Pike. "Quite a literary man, too — writes plays? Clever fellow altogether?"

"Mr. Lancaster is certainly a person of remarkable abilities. He is somewhat wanting in perseverance, perhaps, but he is a man of very versatile talent."

"Exactly. Quite my own impression. Now, I'll tell you what, Mr. Vincent," said Pike, suddenly changing his tone, "he's our man, and I suspected it from the first—at least, perhaps I shouldn't say that, for it was some words you dropped the other day that set me on the right track."

"I?" said Vincent, who had turned very pale.

"Yes—you happened to say you wondered Mr. Lancaster was not present, as you had written to tell him of the circumstances which had occurred, and you knew he was in town. Now he professed to-day to know nothing of the affair."

"It is possible my letter may have miscarried," said Vincent.

"Quite so," said Pike. "Now did you observe—painful business, very—don't wonder you're upset—take a chair, sir—you're standing. Well, now, did you observe Mr. Lancaster, when the blue spectacles were mentioned? He looked perfectly dazed and thunderstruck. He seemed to me to be going to say something, and to stop himself—but that might be merely my idea. But I'm as certain as that I stand here, that he had heard of those spectacles before. That's all I say; I don't pretend to say how or when, yet—but he had heard of them before, sir. And it's a very odd thing, a very odd thing indeed, that his own name should be forged so that he can't tell the difference himself; he told the truth there. I can't either. Now, when you look into 'em, the others are not so very well done—I'll admit so much, though I do represent Dean and Webster —but as for Mr. Lancaster's, I defy any one to suspect it. And it's the hardest to do by far, and it catches the eye the most. Deuced odd, I call it!"

"Mr. Pike," said Vincent, "I cannot for one moment believe you are correct. Mr. Lancaster is a personal friend of my own, and the last person in the world——"

"Of course. Forgers always are. I could tell you queer tales," said Pike. "Of course, it's painful. But if he didn't, who did? Who but a director could have got at the cheques? And then all that's very fishy about the counter-cheques—they tally with the cheques the company meant to draw, but not with these forged ones. It's very fishy indeed! You needn't appear in it, you know. I represent Dean and Webster, and I shall state my opinion. Could you get Mr. Lancaster to step in here, while I just explain my view of the matter to the other directors? I'll do it myself, if you'd rather not. Of course, these things *are* very painful."

CHAPTER XVII.

Who should be trusted now, when one's right hand
Is perjur'd to the bosom?
Two Gentlemen of Verona.

UP to the moment when Pike said, "You'll excuse me, I'm sure, Mr. Lancaster, but certain rules must be observed in an inquiry of this nature; and I must make a statement to the directors, in the exercise of my duty, during which it is better you should not be present"—Horace had been too intent upon a terrible perplexity, which he would not allow to be a suspicion, to notice that his brother directors were a trifle cooler than usual in their manner towards him. But in Vincent's altered looks, more than in a scarcely perceptible peremptoriness in Pike's tone, the conviction flashed into his mind that he himself was under suspicion. He was suspected; and he himself suspected—— But, no! God forbid such a thought as *that*. Horace must have unconsciously groped his way to an easy chair—this was the chairman's private room— he knew he had not fallen; but all was dark, and an oppression which he had felt before (but never to this extent) almost suffocated him. Physical anguish for the moment drowned mental. "If Adelaide could be here, and I could die!" he thought; and then the extremity of pain brought its own antidote, and wrapped mind and body in merciful oblivion.

* * * * *

"Good God! he's dead!" exclaimed Pike, when he, with Vincent and several other directors, returned to inform Mr. Lancaster that they had come to the resolution, in the interests of justice to all parties concerned, to request him to allow his residence to be searched. Some one was running for a doctor, but Vincent stopped him, saying that Mr. Lancaster was subject to fainting fits, which were never of any serious consequence, and that he was coming to.

"I don't believe in fainting fits not being serious," said the director, bluntly. "We can't let the man die, if he *has* done it."

"Wait till he gets home; don't have an *exposé*. We are bound to keep the matter quiet till something is actually proved against him," said Vincent hurriedly.

Meantime, water and wine had been procured, and Horace was sitting up, looking haggard and exhausted, but perfectly collected. He said that he was quite able to go home, if some one would call a hackney coach.

At this, Pike exchanged glances with Vincent, whose self-command could not conceal that he felt his friend's situation most keenly. Pike, who had observed Vincent's anxiety not to fetch in a doctor, thought it possible that Mr. Lancaster's illness was feigned, and that Vincent was not quite to be trusted not to abet an attempt to escape, as he evidently took his position very much to heart.

"It is my painful duty, Mr. Lancaster," said Pike, discharging his delicacy in a nervous cough, "to tell you that there are certain circumstances which seem to make it desirable we should just look over your papers—merely as a matter of form. No doubt everything will be satisfactorily cleared up. You quite understand, I am sure, and so do these gentlemen, that the search is a matter of form. Perhaps you'll allow me and one or two of these gentlemen to come round with you? That will be pleasanter for all parties. Of course, we'll wait till Mr. Lancaster feels himself quite recovered——"

"I am ready to go as soon as you will," said Horace; "the sooner the better."

He wondered at the sound of his own voice. In one of the parts he had played—he could not now remember which—it had sounded like that. He was as calm as he had ever been in his life. That tempest of mental and bodily anguish had swept his soul of passion—almost of the power to feel at all. Just then, he remembered that he was to play *Othello* that night, and old Nollins's odd message about not letting Vincent play *Iago*. Strange that the dotings of an old man should thrust themselves in here; and stranger still that they should almost bring back that dreadful soul-quake which had shaken him just now!

By this time, Horace was mechanically following Pike and the others downstairs. At the turn of the stair he found Vincent beside him.

"Horace," said Vincent, in a low tone (but Pike heard every word), "you believe that I could not have prevented this."

"Depend upon it," thought Pike, as he stepped last into the cab, "he knows that Lancaster did it, and gave him the tip in that letter Lancaster says he didn't receive."

Mrs. Lancaster was out—gone out to lunch. Horace heard it with a sense of relief. She had said that she was going out, but he had forgotten it. He led the way into the library, and, sitting in that same chair in which his father had died, he watched the overhauling of his desk and drawers. The constable in plain clothes, who had ridden on the box, stood stolid but observant near the door. Horace gave up the keys of his deed-box, and of some other boxes containing mostly papers which had belonged to his father. There was nothing to give any clew; all the documents and papers found were easily to be accounted for. There was no sign to be discovered of any recent investment whatever. There were the vouchers for Horace's shares in the Cloppingford Railway Company; but he had bought no new shares for nearly a year, and had always paid up at once. Pike began to think he had been over-hasty, at least, if not on the wrong scent, when, in lifting a bundle of papers out of the deed-box, he came upon something which made him feel like an angler when he has got a bite. Pike plucked one of the directors by the coat-tails as he said carelessly, holding out a pair of blue spectacles—

"Suffered from weak eyes, Mr. Lancaster?"

"No," said Horace. "Those glasses are not mine. I found them in that box a few days ago; but I do not know how they came there."

No one in the room believed him. His manner was constrained; he had never taken his eyes off the box, while Pike was at it, and had no doubt been fearing the glasses would be found.

"I scarcely think, gentlemen," said Horace, unable to bear the tension of silence any longer, "that my being in possession of a very ordinary pair of spectacles justifies this intrusion of my privacy."

Horace knew, before he had finished the sentence, that this was an unwise speech; but it had seemed to him that his silence must needs be revealing some thoughts he dreaded giving utterance to—and surely a little remonstrance was very natural, under the circumstances.

"But this does!" exclaimed Pike. One of the directors had untied the bundle of papers, and was drawing his attention to something. "Look here, gentlemen!" said Pike excitedly. "We are justified, I think, in asking for an explanation of *this!*" He handed it to the others as he spoke.

"You will allow me to see what it is, I presume?" said Horace, with whom indignation was taking the place of far more painful emotions.

"Oh, certainly," said Pike. "But as I think you said you were not near-sighted, you'll excuse me if I don't let it go out of my own hands."

It was the very fac-simile of one of the forged cheques; drawn, like them, on Dean and Webster, and signed with the three names, but it was undated and blank.

CHAPTER XVIII.

So get thee gone; good night!
Othello.

WHEN Adelaide came home, she heard that Mr. Lancaster had brought some gentlemen, who had been a long while in the library, and had gone upstairs, after which they had all gone away together in a cab, as they came.

Horace returned long after his usual dinnerhour. He looked fagged, and said he had had a very fatiguing day. He would tell Adelaide about it to-morrow, but now he must rest a little. He desired her to send him some dinner into the library.

He wanted to be alone, and to think. Until the confusion of his thoughts was less rampant, he could not tell Adelaide. That she would ever doubt him, was a fear which never crossed his mind. He even felt less poignantly than many men would have done the shame in which she must be involved by bearing his name. He had that day been looked upon as a forger and a thief by many men by whom he had hitherto been held in respect, and whose colleague he had been. He, whose pride had been hurt by the thought of his cousin losing by having followed his advice, had had to endure a whole roomful of cold, distrustful eyes. He could see them now—they came between him and the smiling face of his beautiful ancestress, to whose picture he turned for comfort.

He did not believe that any jury would find him guilty—if he took one line of defence. The bare thought of doing so brought back that numbing sensation he had felt in the morning. He would not think of it—yet. At least, not till to-morrow. On the one side stood Adelaide and his children; on the other—— Poor children! they would remember him chiefly as some one whom they must not disturb—his heart reproached him; to-morrow he would turn over a new leaf. To-morrow? To-morrow he was to appear again at the Mansion House; and to-morrow he must tell Adelaide. In the unfathomable misery which seemed to rage around him like an angry sea, he sought an instant's relief in thinking of Theodore and the doctor, who had been sent for to give bail for his appearance next day. Vincent had offered bail, but his bail had been demurred to by Pike, and Horace had himself said he should prefer Dr. Simpson. He had been sure of Theodore's instant and heartfelt sympathy, but the doctor's unhesitating friendship took him by surprise. The doctor had expressed his unshaken confidence in him, in open court, and had begged to serve him in any way. He had promised to come in to-morrow—when Adelaide must know all.

Horace resolved to keep his theatre open as long as possible. His first impulse had been to close it at once; but then he recollected that many of his company would suffer by being suddenly turned adrift in the midst of the season, when they could scarcely hope to meet with other engagements. No, he would keep it open, even though people should come to stare at the actor who was charged with forgery.

Horace was passing through one of the most terrible experiences possible to the human soul—the sudden destruction of the past. A single day had changed the aspect of more than twelve years. Ten thousand memories of those years had become, in one disastrous hour, ten thousand stings of anguish. There was not one of these memories which he must not learn to look at through eyes of doubt and suspicion. And again and again, as in a disordered dream, he strove to guess the secret—if there was one—which his father took away with him into the silence of death. If he could but discover that, all might yet be well.

He had dropped for a moment into a doze, out of which he woke with a start, thinking he heard Vincent's voice saying, " I have never professed to be actuated by any but the universal motive of self-interest, but I assure you it was quite by accident that cheque was slipped into the deed-box."

There was no one there—he had been dreaming. It was late. The room was dark and chilly—the fire nearly out—it flickered on the busts above the book-shelves, but left half the room in darkness. Horace could have sworn that he heard a deep sigh—it seemed to come from the picture, and the superstitious fancy chilled him still more.

He had asked Adelaide to go to the theatre that night. He held her hand as they drove there, but he did not speak, and she always respected his silent moods. She thought, as they went along, that he was still as interesting, and almost as romantically mysterious to her, as when her girlish fancy first strayed towards him. He had for her a kind of double personality; there was the Horace who had something in common with other men, who ate and drank, and would even occasionally (but very rarely) praise a dish; who would take his children on his knee—but this, too, not often—and tell them of his own childhood, and of grandpapa, whose mild blue eyes little Horace had inherited; the Horace who read the *Times*, commented on politics, had had some voice in the making of a railway, and sat beside her in church like any other husband beside any other wife. This Horace could superintend painters and carpenters, be particular in discharging his debts, and in ordering his coats of his tailor. This Horace was grown quite familiar to Adelaide, and there was a certain sense of rest and security in his aspect, a homely pleasure which could be enjoyed without fatigue. A healthy mind returns after a festival to common life with a certain zest, and Adelaide loved this Horace with warm affection. But there was another Horace whom she passionately worshipped. This was the Horace whom she had first loved—the poet and scholar, the man for whom the society around was too tame and prosaic, and who lived in a world of his own, from which he would sometimes step forth, with the glamour of it clinging about him still. This Horace was an inexhaustible poem, with a thousand meanings. She watched him to-night in *Othello*, with as reverent a sense of strangeness as she had felt when she saw him in *Jaffier*, at Dockhampton, years ago. There was no pain in this sense of strangeness; when we trust entirely, it only adds a keener interest that we do not entirely know.

He must succeed at last, thought Adelaide. And he would have succeeded, if he could always have played as he did that night. He had never been so intensely conscious, in one sense—never so unconscious in another. He frightened *Iago* by his terrible looks and tones. Adelaide, shaken with sympathetic passion, was almost as exhausted as he was himself. It seemed only natural that they should drive home as they had come, in utter silence.

CHAPTER XIX.

My place is set too high for aught to touch.
The King and the Angel.

"CHARLOTTE will probably come this morning; so you had better not go out," said Horace, as he rose from breakfast. "I arranged it with Theodore last night."

Adelaide knew by this time that something was wrong, and that the something was connected with the Cloppingford Railway. Horace had been in the City about it all day yesterday, and must go again to-day. Charlotte, when she arrived, knew as much as this, with the addition that Theodore had come home looking as though something dreadful had happened, and had been awake all night she believed. To which Adelaide rejoined that Horace had sat up very late—in fact, almost to morning—and yet had risen rather earlier than usual. Theodore had said that more would be known to-morrow. It was better to wait.

While the women were asking each other what it could be, and wondering whether Horace was really ruined, though he had always said that even the failure of the railway would not quite do that—Horace was surrendering to his bail at the Mansion House. Theodore was waiting for him in the lobby.

The first person he saw in court was Dr. Simpson, whose venerable appearance, and some rumour of his fame which had even reached the ears of the Lord Mayor (through a nephew at Oxford), had procured him a seat on the bench. And in a few minutes Vincent came up, and took Horace's passive hand, saying that all would be well—that something would certainly turn up very soon to release him from this painful, but really ridiculous position. "No one but Pike, who is paid to suspect everybody, and two or three dunder-headed directors, who think you must be shady because you've got a theatre, really think you did it, my dear fellow. It's too ridiculous, you know."

But to this and much more that Vincent said, Horace answered not one word.

Very little was done when the case came on, after two or three hours' waiting. One of Dean and Webster's clerks, who was at home on sick-leave, would return shortly, and it was thought he might have cashed one of the forged cheques. Two other clerks testified that they could testify nothing certainly. Defendant might be the gentleman who presented the cheques in question, or he might not. The clerk who had spoken to a person wearing blue spectacles, was inclined to think defendant too stout—a larger man altogether, but could not swear. So many persons were in and out all day long. It was his business to look at signatures more than faces. He perfectly recollected that cheque. Mr. Lancaster being desired to put on the spectacles, the clerk still said he was a much stouter figure than the man who presented the cheque. Such, at least, was his impression, but he would not swear.

The question of identity entirely broke down; but there was still the blank cheque found in the deed-box to be accounted for—in which cheque, too, the names of Copeland and Vincent were so badly imitated that the inference was that whoever forged those names, would never have ventured to use it. Probably he thought he had destroyed it, added Pike, who drew his worship's attention to these facts. He asked for a remand, to bring more evidence. In a few days the contractor would be able to attend. He might throw some light on the affair.

"Because his name has been forged," muttered Theodore to Horace. "I wonder he does not charge the whole four, Vincent and Copeland as well, with forgery."

Theodore was to look in at the *Portico*, before coming to Russell Square. Horace and the doctor went away together. Vincent had been obliged to leave early.

"Dr. Simpson," said Horace, as the doctor bade him farewell at his own door, "I cannot thank you—I cannot even express in words the support your presence has been to me. But I want to assure you most solemnly, as I am a gentleman and a Christian man, that I am clean in this matter from first to last—whatever be the event, I am innocent. I did nothing, and I knew nothing."

"Nothing shall ever make me doubt it," said the doctor, grasping his hand. "And be sure, my dear sir, that God will bring your innocence to light in due time. Trust in God, my dear sir; and count upon me to do for you to the utmost of my poor ability."

* * * * *

Horace had told his story to his wife and sister in much fewer words than he generally used. He was almost abrupt—he seemed to be stating the case of another man, rather than his own.

"I have often observed how criminals take refuge in ambiguities," he said, when he had told them all, "and by a strange squeamishness about smaller sins, when they have not stuck at greater, allow their innocence to be taken for granted, but avoid a distinct denial. I am not too proud to tell you plainly that I am innocent—I am implicated in no way whatever."

"Oh, Horace, why did you bear it so long? Why didn't you tell me at once?" cried Adelaide in a passion of tears. "My poor darling!"

"I could not speak of it yesterday," he said, stroking her hair—she was kneeling beside him, weeping on his knee.

Charlotte had sat quite still, like one suddenly turned to stone. Horace thought, with something oddly like amusement—in moments of great anguish, the mind seeks trivialities, in self-defence—that his wife and sister had changed characters; it was a new thing for Charlotte to be speechless.

She rose at last, and came to him. Her face was rigid—almost ghastly. He took her hand to support her.

"Horace," she said almost in a whisper, "I know what you suspect—one must say it— Mr. Vincent had been keeping your deed-box for you. And perhaps I can help you. One day last July—on my birthday—I saw him in Piccadilly. He was going into Dean and Webster's, and he had blue glasses on."

There was a strange, forced sound in Charlotte's voice, which alarmed Horace. "My dear girl," he said gently, "are you quite sure of this?"

"Oh, you need not think I mean to perjure myself for your sake," cried Charlotte wildly, "I am positive it was he—I often meant to ask you if his eyes were weak, but I always forgot. Horace! you don't think I'm telling a lie?"

"I did not know what to think—for a moment," he said wearily.

Then he drew her to him, and kissed her, and said that he would go into the library and rest until Theodore came. It was a relief to have told them; but he was tired. Adelaide exclaimed that he must take something—he had eaten nothing.

"In an hour—come to me in an hour," he said; "I shall be better then."

But when, an hour after, they went to bid him come to the dainty little dinner Adelaide had prepared to tempt him, they found him resting more completely than in the brief and troubled snatches of dream-haunted sleep which are the best life knows of repose. Horace lay dead in his chair, with his eyes still lifted to the portrait of *Calliope*, and on his face a deep, inscrutable calm. An hour ago, he looked worn and bowed; but one hour of death had restored his youth. *Othello* lay open on the table, but his face had no look of bitterness, only of solemn and almost triumphant calm.

CHAPTER XX.

> Thrice-tempered steel
> Is not more smooth than he can be—nor hard.
> *Lord and Lady Russell.*

THE world is a cold and a cruel place, and they that dwell therein are hard, unjust, and untrue. While thou doest well for thyself, all men shall speak well of thee, but thou shalt be served like Timon when riches flee away. The world looks at appearances, and troubles itself no further. The world seeks its own, and respects most highly them that do likewise. It despises the honest for their honesty, and hates the good for their goodness. Above all, it hopeth nothing, believeth nothing, and rejoiceth in iniquity. It goes to dine with

Brassheimer at Southumberland Gate, and asks no questions for conscience' sake; but it is very particular to mark its sense of the unscrupulous conduct of John Jones, who embezzled twenty pounds, and was found out before he had even had time to enjoy it.

We are told these things very often (generally by a certain class of persons with a wonderful family likeness); and as most of us think that what a good many people say a good many times must be true, some of us go through life convinced of the injustice of life, and either doubting Providence altogether, or believing that only in the next world do men reap as they sowed. And yet we must all have met with many and many an instance, which might have made us wonder whether there was quite so much injustice in life as we have been taught to believe. There is injustice—there have been, and are, and will be again, crooked things which can never be set straight in the brief span of mortal lives. But in the main, taking life as a whole, there is less injustice than seems. One is sometimes driven to think that perhaps Christianity has after all leavened society, when one hears of the mercy shown to offenders by this same cruel world. How many a young clerk has been forgiven, and tried again? How many a scapegrace has had chance after chance offered him? That divine parable of the Prodigal Son is not only true of the Heart of God—every day we see it true of the heart of man, who was in this, as in other respects, made in the image of God. The fact is, that a wide experience of life inclines one to sympathize considerably with the elder son, who has been held up by divines to opprobrium, because he felt a little aggrieved that no calf had ever been killed to celebrate his never having wasted his father's substance.

We are far too much given to generalizing, and to talking about "the world," as if it were nothing but an aggregate of units. The world is made up of all sorts of people, harsh and gentle, cruel and kind, forgiving and revengeful, tender and cold, false and true. And if we sometimes find that we have thought better of some people than they deserved, we have also found that of others we have not thought well enough. We are quite as often surprised by the faithfulness as by the falsehood of our friends. We have all known, in the persons of others, if not of ourselves, the most wonderful and unfailing kindness, shewn very often to ungrateful and little-deserving people. Yet what of that? Those who shewed the kindness knew that need is a stronger claim than desert; and that *because thou desiredst me* is the divinest reason for either doing or forgiving. And that same poet whose heart it grieved

> " to think
> What man has made of man,"

said, too—

> " I've heard of hearts unkind, kind deeds
>   With coldness still returning;
> Alas! the gratitude of men
>   Hath oftener left me mourning."

It seemed to Adelaide very strange that the world was so full of people, now Horace was gone. After the first despairing agony, she sat among her children—it was more bearable to think of her husband, with her arms round their little necks. Horry understood that papa was gone to heaven, and that mamma was crying because God would not let her go too— yet. " For, of course, mamma, you will go some day, you know. I dare say God thought *I* couldn't let you go yet," he said, stroking her knees in a pretty childish fashion of his own, and looking very gravely into her face. " And I will always be a good boy, and make Dick good too."

Dick was named after Vincent, and Adelaide winced as the child spoke. What was the truth ? What could it be but one thing ? And who would clear Horace's name ?

Mr. Hillyard arrived on the evening of the day following Horace's death. He had seen only the account of the examination at the Mansion House, and had come to town to see if he could be of any service. He was quite overcome on hearing the news. Theodore came down to him and told him all, including Charlotte's immovable persuasion of Vincent's treachery.

"God bless my soul!" exclaimed the honest drysalter, who had been crying heartily. "You don't say so? Why, my poor cousin and he were like brothers!"

"Either he or Horace must have known something about it," said Theodore. "I see no way out of that alternative."

"Of course, we all know my poor cousin Lancaster wasn't the man to do such a thing. But Vincent! Such a superior young man, and behaved so uncommon manly about the will! Well, this is a deceitful world, as my poor mother used to say! But who *would* have thought it?"

"He was always to me an impenetrable man —like a marble wall. I could never see into him, far less see through him. I never saw the real man for a single instant, and I only suspected anything under the surface, because the surface was so smooth and so little troubled by personal feeling of any kind whatever. But I always believed that he threw off the mask with Horace, and was not the impassible statue with him that he was with every one else."

"Some one may have got at the deed-box— one hears queer tales."

"I am quite sure of Vincent's treachery," said Theodore quietly. "I have a friend who writes for a newspaper, and you know newspaper people know each other—at least the little people do. By the merest accident it came out that Vincent has done the dramatic criticisms in the *Express* for years."

"What of that?" said Hillyard, puzzled by his manner. "What's that got to do with his playing my cousin Lancaster false?"

"Only that these criticisms were so disgracefully personal, that Horace always thought they were written by a certain actor with whom he had a quarrel at Dockhampton. You saw him —Willoughby. We all thought he wrote them."

"And you are sure it was Vincent?"

"As sure as one can be of a thing one didn't actually see. And it seems to me now that I ought to have guessed it from his manner. He never expressed any indignation. And these articles exceeded the bounds of criticism—that he was honest in what he said is quite out of the question."

"But I should have thought he'd have pretended to be angry?"

"That was not his way. He is an astuter knave than that. He never pretends anything. I have heard him say a dozen times that he did not profess any exalted virtue."

"Dear, dear!" said Hillyard. "Well, it's an awful business, from beginning to end. Such a very superior young man as he seemed!"

Vincent had called that day, but had been told that the ladies could not see him.

Charlotte had been like one beside herself.

It maddened her to think how little weight her evidence would have, even if she had an opportunity of giving it. What was there to connect Vincent with the crime, in the eyes of any one not enlisted on the other side? And Mr. Meadows had told her—as gently as possible, but yet it seemed a sudden horror —that the coroner's jury would inevitably suspect that a death at such a conjuncture was a suicide. The *post-mortem* examination had revealed heart-disease, but it would be impossible to deny that the disease would probably not have proved fatal for years, but for the intense mental emotion caused by Horace's situation. And even a hint of suicide occurring during the proceedings, and read by every one next day in the newspapers, would go far to fix the question of his guilt in the public mind.

Charlotte listened restlessly. "I will say all I know, if it will be of any use," she said. "But who will believe me?"

CHAPTER XXI.

Gloster. I did not kill your husband.
Richard III.

PEOPLE were always coming and going; there was nothing else to mark the days. Sophia, to whom Charlotte had not confided any of her own private suspicions, spent her time in crying about poor dear Horace, and wishing he had never seen Mr. Vincent's face. The doctor spent long hours alone with Adelaide, and did more than any one else to comfort her. There was so much besides death for which she needed consolation!

On the day of the inquest Mr. Meadows congratulated himself on his foresight in preparing Charlotte, when he heard Vincent called. Vincent's appearance was a surprise to Theodore, who did not know that in a paragraph of the *Express*, which related the "death, under suspicious circumstances, of a railway director," his name had been mentioned as having been present when Mr. Lancaster was taken ill in the board-room. Vincent said, in answer to a question from a juryman, that deceased had occasionally taken a little opium, but did not think that he took it in sufficient quantities, or often enough, to do him much harm—at any rate, not for many months past. Deceased rather prided himself on not being the slave of the habit—he had a great dislike to all forms of over-indulgence, and was a very temperate man. The coroner, having read a note passed to him from Mr. Paston, asked witness whether he had not himself written a prescription of some kind for deceased? Vincent replied that, more than a year ago—in fact, before Mr. Lancaster left Dockhampton—having discovered that he was in the habit of occasionally taking opium, in what he considered to be unwise quantities, he had strongly advised him to lessen the dose, and had written what might be called a prescription; it was designed to cheat Mr. Lancaster into taking a smaller quantity of the drug, and witness believed the design had succeeded.

"Then no other drug of a poisonous nature was contained in your prescription?" asked the coroner.

"Certainly not. The other components were absolutely harmless. I may perhaps state," added Mr. Vincent, "that my father was a medical man, and that I myself once thought of entering the profession, and have a little medical knowledge."

This was quite enough for one of the jurymen. There is such a man on most juries who piques himself on his sagacity, and is always discovering mares' nests, which he insists on his brethren examining. In the present instance, this juryman was convinced that deceased had committed suicide. The motive was obvious. The family, of course, were trying to hush it up. Meadows, who saw the turn things were taking, and knew how all this would read in the report of the inquest, had already sent Theodore for the ladies.

There was a respectful silence when they entered. Adelaide gave her evidence first. Her husband had not been quite well for some months. He had been much depressed at times, but had made no secret of the cause. He was annoyed at some circumstances connected with the *Portico* Theatre, of which he was lessee. Quite lately, within a day or two of his death, there had been another cause—— Here Adelaide almost broke down, but recovering herself said that nothing in her husband's manner indicated excitement. He was calmer than usual; and he had desired her to come to him in an hour. "And he would never, never have bid me come if he had known that I should find him——" Adelaide burst into tears. Theodore would have taken her out, but she would not go. Charlotte meant to say something, and she must hear it.

Charlotte's evidence was to the same effect as her sister-in-law's. But when she had given it, she said, clutching Adelaide's hand, as though the touch gave her strength to speak. "I wish to say, on my oath, that there are several circumstances known to me which leave no doubt at all in my mind as to who is the guilty person."

As Charlotte said this, in a voice which, spite of its trembling, was heard distinctly by every one in the room, she looked at Vincent. He turned livid, and knew that he did; but his nerves were well under control, and he gave no other sign; and if Charlotte had gone on to accuse him to his face, he was prepared to display the utmost allowance for a woman distracted with grief. But she said no more. Adelaide, who knew her sister's intention, had fainted, and Charlotte felt her own endurance failing. Of all the buzz of talking which followed her statement—after one moment's astonished silence, no word reached her brain. By one of those revulsions, common at times of extraordinary excitement, her thoughts busied themselves with another scene which had taken place in that room, when she had wept in Horace's arms for the death of their father. She had sat on that sofa, and Adelaide and Vincent had been there. With such memories the poor overburdened brain tried to cheat itself into a moment's forgetting that Horace lay dead and cold in the next room, and that an hour before there had been a sound of shuffling feet, as the jury went in to "view the body."

There is something primitive in all strong passion. In extreme grief, we become strangely like little children, and reason and knowledge vanish for the time. It seemed incomprehensible to Charlotte, looking on Horace's face, unwasted and unworn, that he could not throw off the slumber which held him so fast that they said he was dead. She almost fancied he could even yet have taken up life once more, if he would but try! Such piteous fantasies torment, and sometimes shock us, but we are not to blame for them. No one—not even those to whom death is The End—has ever sounded the unfathomable pathos of death. Death can come clothed in a solemn triumph—martyrs and heroes may scarcely be wept for with tears. But it is unspeakably pathetic to remember that all human hearts love each other with death standing by, and that we all see each other through a glory of tears.

CHAPTER XXII.

Thee nor carketh care nor slander.
A Dirge.

THE day before the funeral, Adelaide took her two boys into the library, where Horace lay, and bade them kiss him. And then she took them into her own warm living arms, and passionately told them to remember that their father was a good man, and that they must be good for his sake. Little Dick only clung to her, with half-scared eyes, but Horry said in his solemn child's voice, "Mamma, I will. And Dick will. And Lotta will."

Horace was buried beside his father, in the Church of New St. Pancras, in that curious underground burying-place, which not one person in five hundred knows of, of those who daily tread the pavement above.

Theodore felt a thrill of almost superstitious horror on seeing Vincent in the church. Vincent had called every day since Horace's death, but no one had seen him. Theodore intended, if he had had an opportunity, to give as a reason for not having invited him to the funeral, that he was known to have written the criticisms in the *Express;* but Vincent had contented himself with inquiring after the ladies, and had learned from the servants when the funeral would take place.

There were a good many people present. Every one of the *Portico* company was there, and Mr. Kiddle and Mr. Culpepper in particular were observed to be much affected.

"These things make an old fellow like me feel he has no business to be alive," said Meadows to Theodore, as they went down to the vaults.

Theodore never forgot the thrill with which he saw the funeral procession reflected in the looking-glass which hung in the vestry. It happened to hang at such an angle that it reflected not only the figures, but also the winding labyrinths (as they seemed) of the vaults. It was a strange and ghastly sight— the coffin, with its heavy black pall; Doctor Simpson's tall and venerable form, looking like an early Christian Bishop at the funeral of a martyr; the mourners, their faces hidden in their handkerchiefs; and — seeming in the mirror to stand hovering aloof—Vincent, paler than the dead man when they had looked upon him last, but calm and elegant and decorous. Theodore clutched Hillyard's arm, with an involuntary shudder, and hastily glanced round to see whether it were really Vincent, or only the illusion of a disordered imagination. Yes— it was he, but the mirror had lent him that look of the demon, come to see the ruin he had wrought. There was nothing but self-contained decorous grief in Mr. Vincent's aspect as he fell in next to Captain Overton, who was there against his mother's wish.

When the dead had been laid with the dead, and the living emerged once more into the upper airs of the living world, Theodore was thankful to find that Vincent had disappeared. Theodore was fully resolved that he should not return with the others, as an honoured guest, but he had dreaded the unseemliness of an altercation at the door of a mourning coach, and he started to feel a hand laid on his arm, just as they reached the church door. It was not Vincent, however, but Rench, who had never ceased to be Charlotte's solicitor, and with whom Theodore had had some communication since Horace's death.

"Felt I should like to be present on this melancholy occasion, Mr. Paston," said the little lawyer. "I never bore our late lamented client any ill will—never—assure you. Influence, Mr. Paston, influence—that was at the bottom of it all. The only fault of our late lamented client was that he listened a *leettle* too much to what people said. You'll let us know if you come upon anything we could go upon?"

"So far as I can see, there is nothing whatever that could be called evidence——"

"Direct evidence—perhaps not; but I maintain you have strong presumptive evidence. I shall see you in a day or two."

It was very strange and terrible to Adelaide to be sitting in the same room where she had sat eight years ago, on the dreary November afternoon, which seemed to her now to have been the beginning of her life. And now life was ended.

"No, Addy, darling—there are the children," whispered Charlotte. Charlotte had an eager, hungry look; she seemed to be too intensely absorbed in the necessity for action to have time for mere grief. She burst out now and then in wild fits of weeping, but she would soon check herself, as if she were afraid of wasting her strength.

Sophia, who thought they ought to have made an effort to go to the funeral, often jarred sadly on her daughter, and yet perhaps it was better for Adelaide that she should be compelled to realize thus early that life was still going on, though Horace was dead, and that she herself was expected to bear a part in it. And when she found her anguish growing too great, she could always slip away to her children, for whose sake she must bind up her broken heart, and learn to endure the thought of the years to come.

The desire to vindicate Horace's memory had almost dried up Charlotte's tears; and perhaps even Adelaide would have been more prostrated by her grief, had she been like other widows, who have nothing to do but mourn. She had sent little Horry away to the nursery, that he might not hear her mother's allusions to things of which she wished him never to hear, until in years to come she should, it might be, tell him herself— and tell him, she hoped, how his father's name had been cleared. Out of such thoughts as these she would be aroused by hearing her mother saying that one comfort was, Rench would be only too ready to get up a case against Vincent.

Adelaide knew that her husband had made a will, by which he had left Vincent co-trustee with herself for their children, but he had probably destroyed this will on the last night of his life, for it was not to be found, and the rough draft of another, in which Theodore Paston and Dr. Simpson were appointed in Vincent's stead, was unsigned.

Charlotte's statement at the inquest had evidently attracted attention. Theodore had had a letter from Pike on the subject, and had appointed to meet him in Rench's office a few days after the funeral.

CHAPTER XXIII.

My actions shall speak for me.
The Picture.

THE persistent assurances of the few persons who could, by any stretch of the word, be called witnesses, would probably have failed to persuade the would-be prosecutors to consider very seriously the question of Vincent's guilt, had it not been that the terrible collapse in the commercial world—great enough almost to be called the collapse *of* the commercial world—had made all sufferers by fraud even more zealous than usual to discover and punish an offender. Just at that time, too, it was really rather more likely than not that any given man was, to say the least of it, not overburdened with scruples. The greatest and most disastrous collapse of all was yet to be, but quite enough had come to light by the end of 1845 to show that extreme elasticity of conscience was rather the rule in the City than the exception. It is a monstrous thing to be cheated; and companies—which, it is well-known, have neither a soul nor a conscience—resent the picking of their collective pocket almost more keenly than does the individual citizen. And it is even a more monstrous thing that the thief should be at large among us.

Mr. Vincent had undoubtedly been a most efficient director; but so had Dash, Blank, and Stars, all of whom were now snugly lodged in jail for some ingenious little schemes which no one was more astonished to hear of than their brother-directors. And if Mr. Paston's representations were true, it was not at all improbable that Lancaster and Vincent had worked the thing between them. It was pretty plain that Vincent could deal double. Those criticisms in the *Express* proved he was a scoundrel, who could backbite a man all the while he was pretending to be his friend. It was bad—very bad; and probably Vincent was the worst of the two. Poor Lancaster didn't seem the man to contrive a fraud. No doubt was talked into it by Vincent. Think it was a *felo de se*, Mr. Paston? Oh, no, no! Never really thought it was, but Vincent dropped a kind of hint. In fact, now one comes to think of it, he has an uncommon clever way of making one believe a thing, without committing himself to a statement. Very open. Hum, there are a good many ways of being open, Mr. Paston; and Vincent's way is like a man who makes a great parade of letting you see all his empty drawers—takes good care never to let you look into a full one.

By this time, Mr. Moscrop (it was he who had discovered the suspicious cheque among Horace's papers) had fully convinced himself that Vincent was, as he said, "in it," and had probably led astray Mr. Lancaster, who of course was no steadier than he should be, or he would not have turned actor. Mr. Moscrop was a self-made man, and believed himself to be an extreme Liberal, because he disliked the aristocracy. He thought Sir John Overton a pompous old idiot, and could scarcely command his patience when the worthy baronet aired his views at the Board. Sir Saville was even more obnoxious to him. As soon as the affair of the forged cheques got wind, Sir John had expressed, with perhaps injudicious warmth, his determination not to listen to a word against the honour of either Lancaster or Vincent; whereupon Moscrop instantly bethought him that Vincent was son-in-law to one baronet, and brother-in-law (as you might say) to another, and that these aristocratic connections would of course try to hush up the whole thing. Copeland—who had hurried up to town, doubtless at a hint from Vincent, had attempted to ride the high horse over Mr. Moscrop on Vincent's behalf, and Moscrop was beginning to feel it might be his not altogether unpleasant duty to maintain that glorious Charter on which he had descanted at more than one Mechanics' Institute, and to prove to his admiring countrymen that in England no rank or title can protect a criminal from justice.

Vincent heard, with perfect self-possession, that suspicion was considered to attach to himself. He looked pale and grave, but scarcely anxious, and merely remarked that he reserved his defence for the present. Sir John became bail for him, and brought him in his own carriage to the Mansion House as often as he appeared there. Slightly differing varieties of the same case were very common about that time—Vincent was not the only chairman accused of having abused his opportunities; but an especial interest was excited in him by the circumstances attending Horace Lancaster's death, as to which many conflicting rumours were current.

Vincent engaged no counsel. His questions to the witnesses were few, and eminently judicious. In spite of the utmost efforts of

Mr. Lancaster's friends and Mr. Vincent's enemies (among whom Vincent took care the Court should know Rench must be reckoned, with the reason therefor), it seemed at first that very little fresh evidence was to be discovered, and none at all which was incompatible with Horace's complicity. There was a sensation in Court when Mr. Paston said, in answer to Rench's questions, that Mr. Vincent had written a series of scurrilous attacks on his friend's acting, in the *Express*. But the editor of the paper professed entire ignorance, and the sub-editor sent a certificate of sickness, and his worship thought the time of the Court should not be wasted on irrelevant matters like these.

That clerk of Dean and Webster's, however, who had gone home on sick-leave, and whom Rench took care to examine before the Court had got over the unfavourable impression created by Mr. Paston's evidence had subsided, inclined to think Mr. Vincent was the person who had changed a cheque on the 9th of July;

and when Mrs. Paston was called to prove that on that very day she saw Vincent go in to Dean and Webster's Bank, Rench surreptitiously rubbed his hands for joy. Charlotte looked pale and ill—she glanced once at Vincent, who never removed his eyes from her. It was by a great effort that she preserved her self-control—those who stood near the accused fancied that he, too, was more nervous than usual while this witness was being examined. Rench put the questions, and went into the intimacy between Mr. Lancaster and Vincent, and the entire trust reposed by the former in the latter, together with the fact that, on the day before his death, Mr. Lancaster had destroyed a will which made Vincent trustee for his widow and children. Rench also drew from Charlotte all that she knew about the deed-box. He then questioned her closely on what every one in Court felt to be the most important point of all—the matter of Vincent's identity with the person she had seen entering the Bank.

Charlotte's evidence was clear enough as far

as it went. There was no doubt about the date—the 9th of July was her birthday, and she had come up from Twickenham to meet her husband, and go with him to choose a birthday gift. Being asked if she was quite sure that it was Vincent whom she saw, Charlotte replied that she was as sure as one can be from seeing a person without speaking to him, and added that she should certainly have spoken, if she had come up with the person she saw before he turned into the Bank. While Rench examined her, she spoke with the calmness of desperation, but all the faces in Court seemed to be blurred together into a hazy background, from which Vincent's pale face and deep-set eyes stood out terribly distinct. She dared not look at him, and yet felt irresistibly drawn to look. It was with infinite relief that she somehow understood (for she was so agitated that she could not hear the words he uttered) that he did not intend to ask the witness any questions. But she had scarcely sunk trembling on the seat to which Theodore led her, when Vincent said, as if by an after-thought, "By permission of the Court, there is one question I should like to ask the witness." Charlotte's heart died within her, and her brain seemed to reel, but she rose instantly and returned to the box, with one imploring glance at her husband, who could only whisper, "Courage!"

"I should like to ask the witness," said Vincent with perfect courtesy and self-possession—in curious contrast to the very evident flutter of the witness, "whether she mentioned to any one that she had seen me?"

No, she had intended to mention it, but when her husband returned that night, he brought news which made her forget all about it.

"May I ask the nature of the news?"

"It was connected with the *Portico* Theatre."

"With the financial department?"

"Yes," answered Charlotte, desperately perceiving the drift of the question.

"And of so disturbing a nature that you

forgot to tell your husband, or any one else, that you had seen me? And never mentioned the circumstance until you heard that forgeries had been committed on Dean and Webster?"

"Yes."

"Your memory is precise, Mrs. Paston," said Vincent, so gravely that no one could have called his tone sarcastic. "Do you happen to remember how long a time intervened between the return of the deed-box which has been mentioned—your brother's deed-box—and the finding of the forged blank cheque by Mr. Moscrop, on the 20th of October?"

Charlotte thought it was about ten days.

Mr. Vincent quietly remarked that he had no further question to put to the witness, and Charlotte was once more leaving the box, when Rench, jumping up rather hastily, exclaimed, "One moment, Mrs. Paston—is there any doubt in your own mind that you saw defendant, as you have described, on the 9th of last July?"

"None whatever," said Charlotte steadily, looking at Vincent this time. And Vincent having been made, at Rench's suggestion, to put on the blue spectacles, she again declared her conviction to be unshaken.

In his address to the Court, Vincent showed considerable acumen—and more perhaps in what he did not say, than even in what he did say. He skilfully passed over everything which more immediately affected Horace Lancaster, and Pike was more than ever convinced that he was trying to screen his friend's memory. Most outsiders were very favourably impressed by Vincent's gentlemanly bearing, and by the great moderation of his defence, and a whisper got about that he could disprove the charge against himself in a moment, if he would only sacrifice his friend.

Vincent began by an expressive allusion to the painful position in which he was placed. It was his misfortune, he said, to find himself in that position, at a juncture when it was almost impossible that his case should be heard with all the impartiality on which Englishmen so justly pride themselves. At a great commercial crisis, when the most nefarious schemes were being daily brought to light, he felt that, in the minds of most persons, any man arraigned on such a charge as this was more or less involved in the suspicion and obloquy attaching at the present moment to every man who was, or who appeared to be, in any way connected with the circumstances and transactions which had led to the present unhappy complications. Many worthy persons would perceive in the very words, "railway director," grounds for distrust—and almost for condemnation. But such a state of feeling could be but transient, and Mr. Vincent confidently awaited the time, not far distant, when the directors of the Cloppingford Railway, at least, would be triumphantly exonerated from all participation in the unjustifiable courses to which so many had unhappily lent themselves. Mr. Vincent challenged the closest investigation into the position of the company he had the honour to have served to the best of his poor abilities. His brother-directors knew that he had consistently opposed more than one indiscreet proposal, which, if carried out, might now have involved the company to some extent in the nearly universal condemnation. The Cloppingford Railway Company had stood its ground during a crisis which had shaken the commercial world to its foundations; and he appealed to his brother-directors to say whether his own counsels had helped or hindered this happy result.

Here Mr. Copeland cried, "Hear, hear," and drummed with his umbrella, and was called to order. Sir John, who had perceived his action, imitated it, and being extremely deaf was with difficulty reminded that he was not in the House, and must suppress these exhibitions of sympathy. Meanwhile Mr. Vincent was going on to say that he made full allowance for the irritation of his brother-directors, who, at a time when an unfavourable whisper might bring about a disastrous panic, saw their company's credit injured by the revelation of a system of fraud, which until the perpetrator was discovered threw a cold shade of suspicion over every one ever so little in the company's confidence.

Vincent treated the accusation against himself as almost too unfounded to be noticed. He had, he observed, but little difficulty in accounting for it. The Court had heard from more than one witness that he had had the misfortune to incur the displeasure of the late Mr. Lancaster's family solicitors.

"Your worship, I protest against such an insinuation!" cried Rench, struggling to his feet in spite of Pike's attempt to hold him down by the coat-tails. "Such an observation is capable of but one interpretation, and that interpretation I utterly repudiate!"

Mr. Vincent observed that his words were not intended to insinuate that any one of the prosecution was guilty of intentionally wronging him. But he repeated that he had been the cause of a wealthy client withdrawing his affairs from Messrs. Lambton, Rench, and Lambton, and he left the Court to draw its own conclusions. As regarded the forgeries themselves, he would only remark that it was admitted that his own signature was so badly imitated that the wonder was it had not caught the attention of the cl——

"No, no, we don't admit that," said Pike. "We only say that when we know it's a forgery, we can detect several little differences, whereas Mr. Lancaster's would defy any-one——"

"At any rate," said Vincent, "if the other names had been as badly done as mine was, we should have discovered the fraud months before we did. The one piece of evidence against me," continued Vincent in a constrained but scarcely embarrassed voice, "is the fact that Miss Charlotte Lancaster—I mean Mrs. Paston—has said she saw me, on a certain day in July, entering Dean and Webster's Bank, and wearing spectacles resembling those which the Court has had the opportunity of examining. On that point, I will say nothing."

Mr. Vincent paused for a full minute before he went on to observe that the clerk's evidence went no further than "thinking" that he might be the man. "That is," said Vincent, "he remembers nothing to prove that I am not the man. On that point I will say no more. But an attempt has been made to shew that my unfortunate friend Mr. Lancaster saw reason, in the very last hours of his life, to withdraw his confidence from me—and hence it is insinuated that he knew something to my disadvantage. Other insinuations have been made, equally cruel. By adding a little, taking away a little, misrepresenting a little, and exaggerating a little, my conduct towards my unhappy friend has been set in an odious light, in order to destroy my credit. There is no evidence that I have committed forgery; so an attempt is made to blacken even my efforts to serve my unhappy friend. These aspects of the case are fraught to me with more pain than either those who accuse me or those who defend me can know. I do not stand here to defend my conduct towards my unfortunate friend; but I owe it to myself, and to a wife and children, who are as dear to me as yours, gentlemen, are to you——" Here Vincent looked at Moscrop and Sir John; and Sir John, who heard not one word, mumbled "Hear, hear." "I owe it to them not to allow one statement to pass unnoticed. It has been said—nay, sworn—that my unhappy friend destroyed a will, which appointed me the legal guardian of his family. That will was not destroyed; it was committed to my charge. I have sent for it."

At this moment Charlotte saw Mr. Vincent's servant trying to make his way through the crowd.

"This is my reply to the statement which has been made, your worship," said Vincent, handing a document to the clerk of the Court. "If the passage which I have indicated may be read, the Court will be better able to judge whether Mr. Lancaster had revoked his confidence in me. The will is not yet proved—my painful position caused the delay."

The document was carefully examined. It was dated more than a year ago, and was quite in order. The passage Vincent referred to ran thus:—

And I give and bequeath to Richard Vincent Esq. Member of Parliament barrister-at-law the sum of ten thousand pounds to be paid duty free in shares of the Cloppingford Branch-line Railway Company such shares now standing in my name as a small token of my gratitude for the inestimable services he has rendered me And I appoint the said Richard Vincent Esq. to be along with my wife Adelaide the guardian and trustee of my children until my sons shall respectively attain the age of twenty-one years and my daughter shall attain that age or shall marry And I desire that the said Richard Vincent shall administer my worldly affairs after my death and at his discretion invest or re-invest my moneys as shall seem good to him for the benefit of my said wife and children the said Richard Vincent not to be liable for any loss which may unavoidably occur in such investments or re-investments.

The reading of this passage made a considerable sensation, but there was almost as much difference of opinion about it as about the more serious issue. Some were more than ever shocked at Vincent's perfidy towards his confiding friend; but others thought it not impossible that the criticisms of which so much had been made (and whose malignity had doubtless been greatly exaggerated), were written with Lancaster's knowledge, and as a kind of left-handed puff. There are tricks in all trades, said these knowing ones, and such things have been done before now.

Vincent was so far right in his estimate of the effect of the public agitation, that the case against him would probably have been dismissed at any other time. As it was, he was committed to take his trial at the next sessions. While the buzz of voices went on round him—Pike, Moscrop, and Rench, each offering a different argument why bail should not be taken, Vincent stood immovable, one hand thrust into his breast, and the other holding Horace's will. Adelaide, sitting with Dr. Simpson in the least conspicuous corner of the Court, watched him with fascinated eyes. The doctor had taken her hand when that passage was read, by which Horace had left her and her children in Vincent's power; he held it still, and Adelaide clung to him as a drowning man clings to the succouring rope.

"Your worship will accept the sureties if the amounts are doubled?" said Sir John rather testily, adding in a loud aside, of which Moscrop got the benefit, "Why, demmy, Copeland, I can't let a son-in-law of mine go to jail, can I?"

CHAPTER XXIV.

Since the world was made,
Did evil never truly conquer good,
But only seemed to conquer.
Lord and Lady Russell.

MR. VINCENT was never required to surrender to his bail. The Grand Jury ignored the bill; and Mr. Moscrop in disgust retired from the company, and never made a speech as long as he lived without bringing in some allusion to that truckling to the aristocracy and their connections, which is a disgrace to our liberal institutions.

After a brief period of depression, the Cloppingford Railway Company became more flourishing than ever. A deputation, headed by Sir John and Mr. Copeland, waited on

Vincent with a handsome testimonial, and an equally handsome expression of sympathy, indignation, and confidence. Those of the directors who did not concur, either held their tongues or followed Moscrop's example ; and Vincent managed the affairs of the company for some years in a manner which convinced his admirers of the utter groundlessness of the charge against him, and of their own courage and wisdom in standing by him. Had not malicious charges been brought against Mr. Hudson himself ?

Charlotte was at first for disputing Horace's will, but even Rench gave his voice against this. And Vincent decided the question for them, long before the Grand Jury was empanelled which threw out the bill against him. He sent the will to Lambton, Rench, and Lambton, who, he understood, were acting for Mrs. Lancaster, and with it a note, in which he said that under the painful circumstances which had occurred it would be impossible for Mrs. Lancaster to act with him on the terms which ought to subsist between co-trustees. He should be happy to serve Mrs. Lancaster in any possible way, but felt that, under the circumstances which had arisen, the only course open to him was to decline to act as trustee.

On this side time, this was the end. No more was discovered. Surmise and doubt never became certainty. The tragedy of life does not always culminate in a visible catastrophe. At first, Vincent would seem to have come safely, if not quite triumphantly, out of the affair. *Not proven* is a verdict which leaves something to be desired; but as no one else had been proved guilty, Vincent's innocence might be considered to be merely the unprovable negative of logicians. So convinced was Mr. Copeland of this, that by his last will he left Vincent ten thousand pounds (to the extreme disapproval of his nephew and heir), "as a mark of my confidence in his integrity, and of my admiration of his talents."

For all this, however, as time went on, the

belief in Horace's entire innocence deepened in the minds of all who had ever known him. Perhaps his widow's scrupulous discharge of all claims upon him, and her generous behaviour to the *Portico* company aided in producing this effect. But it would almost seem as if there were some inherent virtue in mere lapse of time, to clear our mental vision, and enable us to judge more truly. We have all probably been sometimes surprised, on looking back, to see how much more comprehensible to us things and persons have become. When the irritation of public feeling had subsided, and the confusions of too great nearness were lost in distance, every one who had known Horace Lancaster told himself and his friends that he had always felt the idea was preposterous— Lancaster was no more the man to do a thing of that sort than—than—in short, the directors must have been crazy, if indeed they were not purposely misled by the guilty party. Who this guilty party was, did not transpire; but somehow time did not seem to be convincing people that Vincent was not the man to do a thing of that sort.

Those who knew the facts, knew that he and Horace Lancaster could not both be innocent, and felt more certain every year that they were not equally guilty. Those who did not know the facts, but had heard that there was " something which had never been cleared up," felt that so inscrutable a man as Vincent would hardly have been suspected at all had he been innocent. Only Mr. Copeland, Sir John, and Amelia believed that Vincent had refrained from vindicating himself more fully, in order to spare his friend's memory. Upon the whole, Vincent attracted very little enthusiasm, and many a bungling villain has found more people ready to swear to his innocence. Perhaps had he maintained the attitude of cynical candour, which he had at first affected (it is an admirable mask, especially adapted to deceive the feebler sort of honest folks), he would have been more popular. But he seemed to feel that moral sentiments were required from a man who had been suspected of a grave immorality, and in his later life he adopted a tone of strict respectability, which was much less interesting. Amelia always believed that that unhappy affair of poor Mr. Lancaster's had broken her husband's heart, for she was quite sure he was never the same after it.

When all claims were discharged, Adelaide found herself left with very little more than the legacy which her uncle had bequeathed to her, which had been settled on her at her marriage, and which Horace had always refused to invest in railway shares. When Rench came to investigate his late client's affairs, he discovered that some very large sums had unaccountably disappeared. The vouchers for a great number of the shares in the Cloppingford Railway were not to be found. It appeared that they had been sold, but when and by whom was a mystery which Rench explained in his own way. Enough shares had been retained to make a considerable addition to Adelaide's means, in after years, when the traffic on the Cloppingford Branch-line exceeded even Mr. Vincent's promises; but at present there was not enough left of Horace's fortune to educate his children as he had wished, and to keep up the house in Russell Square. Dear as it was to Adelaide, she had never had time to make it what we mean by home, and she was not altogether sorry that she could not remain in a house which was full of so many memories. She herself felt that there the past would assert itself too strongly above the present. It would be hard to do anything there but sit with her children at her knee, listening for the footsteps that would come again no more. The doctor entreated her to make his house the home of her widowhood, and she consented—at first, for her children's sake, but very soon she found that she, too, was less lonely for the loving and fatherly care which never failed. They were seldom separated; when the doctor returned to Oxford, Adelaide and her children accompanied him—the good doctor deriving much pleasure from the thought that the lads would acquire a love for learning by breathing the classic atmosphere.

Poor Sophia caused Adelaide most of the pain she suffered, for many years after the one great sorrow made most other pain of little account. Sophia could not refrain from referring to Vincent, and all the evil which she, at any rate, believed he had brought upon her and hers. Sophia had a wrong of her own to complain of—during that brief depression, she sold her shares at a tremendous loss, and she never bought a new bonnet or gown without lamenting, first, that she ever put her money into those speculating concerns, and then that she ever took it out. It is recorded that when the fact came to the doctor's knowledge, his usual ascetic austerity was overcome for the moment. The good doctor very often smiled, as Adelaide's children well knew, but on this occasion, Caleb asserted that he laughed.

"Not when missus told him, I don't mean, Mrs. Staples," he explained to that worthy woman. "But I heard him a-laughing to himself in his study."

Caleb had little cause to make merry over Mrs. Simpson's misfortunes, for he had disposed of his own shares in as great a hurry, and at as great a loss, as his mistress. The next time that the doctor paid Caleb his wages, he asked him how much he had lost by putting his money into railways.

"A matter o' two hundred an' fifty pound, sir, or thereabouts," said Caleb, shifting uneasily beneath the doctor's eye.

"Ah, you had better have followed Mr. Bolland's advice, Caleb. As the wise king saith, 'Wealth gotten by vanity shall be diminished: but he that gathereth by labour shall increase.'"

Caleb hung his head, and looked foolish.

The doctor waited six months, and then told him that he had paid two hundred and fifty pounds in his name, into the Bank of England —"Of which," observed the doctor, "it may be said with some degree of truth, that there thieves do not break in and steal."

The doctor did not make up Sophia's losses, but he was liberality itself in all other respects, and she was able to pay a visit to Bath once a year, in the season. During one of these visits she caught a cold, which brought on a quinsy of which she died. When she could scarcely speak, she expressed her gratitude and affection to the doctor in a manner which deeply moved him.

"I've been a sad worldly woman," said poor Sophia; "it's very hard for a woman *not* to be worldly. I hope you'll think of me as kindly as you can. I wish I could have been more like you."

The doctor mourned her very sincerely; but Adelaide and her children were left to him, and he often said that his last days were his best days.

Theodore made himself a name in Germany. His opera of *Undine* has been heard with delight in Vienna itself, and a great musical critic said of his works, that one did not know how great they were until one heard the music of lesser men. "We can always criticize little works," added the critic. "But we forget to criticize great ones, until we come to compare them with others."

To both Theodore and Charlotte it was an abiding grief that Horace's name was never publicly vindicated. But there came a time when a reaction set in strongly against even successful speculation, and when the Railway King himself found his throne crumbling beneath him. The lustre of Vincent's reputation grew somewhat tarnished about the same time. It was said that he was angling for a baronetcy, and had been feathering his nest by means similar to those whereby Mr. Hudson admitted that, "on paper," he seemed to have netted thirty-eight thousand pounds. However it was—and no one knew exactly how it was—Vincent retired, and Sir Saville Fidelle was made chairman in his stead. Vincent however who had been re-elected for Cloppingford, bore the somewhat ungrateful conduct of the company with much philosophy, made a considerable figure in Parliament, and took an active part in the first Great Exhibition, in the railway-machinery department of which he was considered an authority. But on the whole he was perhaps a disappointed man. His large fortune (which he was understood to have acquired chiefly by successful speculation in railways) did not bring him so much eminence as many far poorer men attained; and even his talents went for less than they deserved. Perhaps he lacked the capacity for illusion— an inestimably useful thing in a world like ours. There is a saying attributed to Cromwell, that *a man never climbs so high, as when he does not see where he is going.* Richard Vincent always saw where he meant to go, and he believed that he aimed higher than most men, and saw more clearly; but he found too late, that somehow or other the men he had despised had climbed higher than he, and he lived to hear Horace Lancaster spoken of (by persons ignorant of the connection between him and Vincent), as a man in advance of his age, who, had he but lived to mature his genius, would have left an abiding fame.

THE END.

www.ingramcontent.com/pod-product-compliance
Lightning Source LLC
Chambersburg PA
CBHW032057220426
43664CB00008B/1034